WEB 2.0

I0004662

Civic Media in Action –
Emerging Trends & Practices

Alan R. Shark & Susan Cable

PUBLISHED BY PUBLIC TECHNOLOGY INSTITUTE • ALEXANDRIA, VIRGINIA

Civic Media in Action – Emerging Trends & Practices

Published by:
Public Technology Institute
1426 Prince Street
Alexandria, Virginia 22314
www.pti.org

Printed in the United States of America

ISBN 13: 978-1463530815
ISBN 10: 1463530811

Preface

Web 2.0 continues to impact our society in ways that were never thought possible. State and local governments have been highly innovative in experimenting with Web 2.0 and social media technologies as a means of better informing and engaging citizens. At the same time, many others continue to struggle, for a variety of reasons, to figure out the best strategies for their jurisdictions. We all recognize that we are embarking on rather new and untested technologies and their potential impacts. Add to the equation the fact that many localities lack the expertise, training, budget, equipment, and understanding of the required policies and procedures–there is a desperate need to share in best practices and expand the ever-growing knowledge base.

This book is designed for those seeking to learn more and understand all that is involved in civic media using Web 2.0 technology.

The Public Technology Institute, now 40 years young, has been on the forefront of thought leadership in the area of Web 2.0 and social networking – that we often refer to as civic media. Thanks in part to the support of the Alfred P. Sloan Foundation for their initial underwriting of this book, as well as support for our *Web 2.0 State & Local Awards Program* and our *Citizen Engaged Communities Designation Program*. In particular, I want to thank the Foundation's program officer, Ted Greenwood, for his strong support in this new area of citizen empowerment and engagement. He began supporting such projects in this area going back a decade before they became popular or even known.

We are also grateful to Susan Cable, who has been our lead project manager and lead researcher over the past three years and who was the major contributor to this book. Without her knowledge, dedication and enthusiasm, this project would not have been possible.

It is our hope to continue updating this book periodically, as there is new information every day that can only add to the text. Moreover, we encourage readers to turn to PTI's website and Facebook page to keep abreast of the latest activities in civic media.

According to a PEW 2010 study,[1] among the population as a whole, when faced with a question, problem or task that requires contact with government, 35 percent prefer calling on the phone. While moving forward with new technologies and new applications for new devices, governments must recognize this gap, or preference, that exists in the adaptation and utilization of new media. We all have experienced that service issue for which the only action we wanted to take was to speak to a live person about the problem. So, as governments progress in adding new communication channels and platforms to citizen interactions and engagement, they must continue to ensure the availability of multi-channel options to truly achieve democratic governance, acknowledging the needs of all demographics.

Finally, in the interactive society in which we live, please send us items that we may have missed and let us know what you would like to see covered next time!

Table of Contents

CHAPTER 1

Web 2.0 and Beyond

Web.2.0 is a term that has been used for some years now, and while the term itself has not changed, the concept has evolved and continues to adjust every day. Looking back in time, we seemed to skip over Web 1.0 as many navigated the Web for the first time and where happy to just get online and send an e-mail. Today there are hints by thought leaders as to what Web 3.0 and beyond might look like. With Web 2.0 however, there is no shortage of descriptions and definitions, they all point to some common characteristics, which include:

- Interactive
- Web-based
- Browser-based
- Intuitive
- Content Sharing
- Content development by users
- Collaboration tools
- Interactive games
- Applications
- Mobile applications

Function and Usage

In terms of functions, Web 2.0 includes elements such as **Searching**, **Linking**, **Authoring**, **Podcasting**, **Blogging**, **Media** and **Social Networking**. All of this is wholly dependent on a vibrant and open information data system called the Internet, or The World Wide Web. Katie Couric at a recent commencement address at Boston University said, "The beauty of Web 2.0 is that everyone has a voice and the negative to that is everyone has a voice!" On the later point, she was referring to the fact that we see so much civil discourse and uncivil behavior, and quite frankly, ignorance.

With the growth of the Internet exceeding all expectations, it's no surprise they ran out of internet protocol (IP) addresses, which is akin to running out of telephone numbers.

Knowing this would happen sooner than later, the powers that be had already prepared for the moment with an exceedingly robust new number assignment system called IPv6, which replaced the now depleted IPv4. There really never was an IPv5 for reasons that do not pertain to this book. The new and richer addressing system is automatic to the average user, but it does provide dramatic growth for new applications and uses. As illustrated in Figure 1, today there are over two billion people on the Internet worldwide.[2] By the close of 2010 there was a 77.4 percent Internet penetration rate in North America. Web 2.0 and civic/social media technologies can be utilized as dynamic tools for informing the public about issues impacting the community, encouraging collaboration for improved communications and service delivery, and engaging the public in government decision-making.

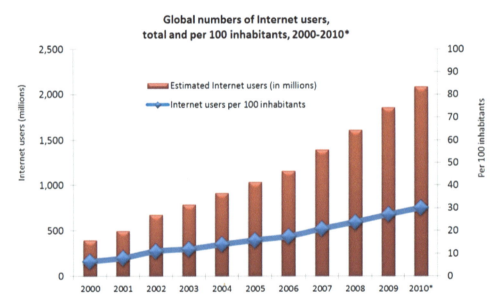

Figure 1. ITU

While social networking is only a derivative of Web 2.0, the two terms are most often used synonymously. Today we find ourselves navigating into new territory, where old laws no longer apply, and new rules have yet to be written. Navigating through pages of websites and webpages we now have new choices where we may click for a page or click for an application. We may choose among widgets, bookmarks, applications, buttons, tabs and more. Web 2.0 and social networking has many new outlets and new devices with a major shift toward mobility.

Prior to 2004, the likes of Twitter, Facebook, and YouTube did not exist. As this book goes to press, Twitter has over 200 million registered users who send out over 65 million Tweets per day. Facebook, founded in 2004, has over 600 million users where the average user has 130 "friends", where collectively people spend over 700 billion minutes per month. Facebook is translated into 70 languages, and 70 percent of its users reside outside of the United States.

When it comes to the growth of mobile devices (smart phones, PDA, and tablets), Facebook has over 250 million active users. Today, there are at least 200 mobile operators in over 60 countries working to deploy Facebook mobile products; making this one of the fastest growing market segments.

YouTube, now owned by Google, was created in 2005. Their slogan "Broadcast Yourself" resonates in over 34 supported languages. Each day, over 24 hours of video are uploaded every *minute* and enjoys over two billion visits per day. It would take 1700 years to watch each and every video, and of course that number expands exponentially each day. The average user spends 15 minutes per day on YouTube, as over 100 million video clips are viewed daily. These are staggering numbers to digest. All this continues to evolve and grow, and it's difficult to tell what will be the big new names and applications for tomorrow.

The Government Setting

When it comes to Web 2.0 and social media in the state and local government setting, public managers are challenged as never before to literally 'expose' themselves to an uncertain yet demanding public. The challenge ahead is not only to figure out how best to embrace the new web-centricity in one's personal life – but to figure out the enormous power, pitfalls, and possibilities that can be integrated in one's professional life. When it comes to government websites and mobile applications, this requires much time in planning and staking out new policies and procedures, as well as experimentation, exploration, and careful navigation.

Today's city or town hall may look the same from the outside but the ways we connect with government and one another have forever changed. The Internet and its emerging social media sites and tools have helped change the landscape and focus to a new and unchartered cyber landscape where boundaries and interests are no longer confined by mere physical structures. They say all politics is local, as most citizens tend to identify with local governments that are closer to home – even if they are surfing their "home" city website 3,000 miles away.

E-Government was a term that helped explain that many government functions were posted or found on a local government website. This meant that the public now had a place to check on basic information, such as hours of operation and the names and phone numbers of key public managers and leaders. As e-government advanced, it is now commonplace to pay for certain administrative functions such as parking fines, building permits, pet licenses, park permits, etc., online. No longer satisfied as a timesaving, efficient, one way conduit of broadcasted information, the monolithic website has morphed into a new construct, where the home page becomes a launch pad – not a lone destination page. Today we hear public leaders and citizens calling for compelling power terms such as *transparency, citizen empowerment,* and *citizen engagement.* This will enlarge the potential of government Web 2.0 and emerging social media applications.

Traditionally, most citizens have received news about government largely from the print media, but there is a diminishing role for newspapers, as we have known them. We know that overall print media circulation is down and declining. We also know that depending on locality, citizens are turning to their local government websites to either find out about something or to fill out a form and perhaps pay by credit card for a particular service. Local governments, after all, are usually the first place where a citizen might turn. Moreover, local government websites largely are in a constant state of improvement in terms of providing information, making it easier to navigate, providing greater opportunities to complete certain transactions online as opposed to standing on line. In a few short years, we have moved from merely posting information to transacting information, to allowing citizens to react to certain events and measures – to actually seeking two-way citizen engagement.

Communication Channels—Challenges and Opportunities

Until recently, citizens learned about what was going on in their community and local government through newspapers and television. Now there is a major shift from printed newspapers where circulation continues to decline yet online news is beginning to grow. According to the Annual Report on American Journalism, over 26 percent or one out of four Americans now get their news delivered to their smart phones – many instead of their front door. No doubt, that number will certainly continue to rise. Perhaps not surprisingly, the study also finds that the Internet has become the third most popular news source.

Unlike Web 2.0 functionality, social media sites can provide a high degree of interactivity and user generated content (UGC). This is still an area where more work needs to be done. First, not everyone agrees with what citizen engagement means. To some, it means to provide citizens with the opportunity to comment on a specific issue. Others see it quite differently, where interactivity and content development is both encouraged and processed. For example, a police chief from a small jurisdiction in the Midwest was complaining that some younger residents were sending in pictures from auto accidents and fires wanting to be helpful. He was upset that they were upset that the police and fire dispatch departments had no way to capture and process the photographs and therefore it was not helpful at all. This is an example of a growing disconnect regarding how technology is being used and will increasingly be used by our citizens. If we want to engage citizens, it will certainly need to be done so with knowing the state of technology, as well as the devices citizens are most comfortable in using. When it comes to devices, the cell phone has emerged as a very smart device that is truly nothing less than a feature-rich pocket computer with a phone as an application.

There is no such thing as a dumb wireless phone – it is just that some are getting much smarter. Tablet devices such as the iPad, and others using the Android operating system, with their rich user interface simply make it easier to get and respond to information. They come equipped with ever-larger high definition screens and without any external pointing device or cumbersome keyboard. New pocket cameras are on the market that not only takes great shots, they record the time and date, latitude and longitude, (geotag) which has the potential to take the concept of neighborhood watch to entirely new levels. Engagement then is more interactive, as compared to transparency, with citizens having the ability to actually produce content as opposed to merely viewing it. The new content can be in the form of opinions, new ideas, reactions to other's ideas, pictures, video, and much more.

Social media is better geared toward civic engagement and we are now seeing the start of an emerging civic engagement ecosystem in cyberspace. The "mobile device", be it a smart phone, tablet, laptop or other medium, has for most citizens become the central means of communicating two-way information; facts as well as opinions; text as well as photos and videos.

Transformation through Technologies

The value of Web 2.0 technologies and social media tools for government is becoming more evident, as the transformation of today's communication channels is increasingly affecting how public institutions function and deliver services.

Used effectively, Web 2.0 and civic/social media encourage citizens to take a more active role in local and state government. They provide a platform to streamline government communications and services through knowledge bases, access to networked resources, real-time data communications and reporting, wireless access, multi-media delivery, integrated self-service options, location-based services and cross-agency information sharing.

State and local governments have evolved along with their citizens from e-government to m-government and have moved away from a web-centric model to a multi-channel approach. While websites continue to serve an invaluable purpose of providing key information and offering online services and payments, they are now moving to the mobile device be it a smart phone, a laptop, or a tablet as another way to reach and engage its citizens. The term mobile applications (apps) is a relatively new channel of communication. Apps, as they are called, may exist and operate entirely outside a local government's operations and website. They might take the form of a stand-alone applications or be fully integrated into a local government's communications center.

Public managers are increasingly looking at new ways to engage the public as a means of improving communications and restoring trust. We know, for example, that at the end of 2010, there were 302,947,098 mobile phones or 97.4 percent penetration. The research firm Nielsen predicted that 2011 would be the year when smart phone penetration would surpass regular mobile phones. However, this prediction was offered before the unexpected and explosive growth of the iPad tablets and all the competing tablets that emerged as a result. With iPad2 and other tablet growth, website developers are already being forced to rethink their website designs and functionality in order to best accommodate this new mobile device medium.

With all the growth in local government outreach using social/civic media comes many disappointments. In 2010, the Public Technology Institute (PTI) conducted a national survey directed to those who manage their social media applications asking about how they were using the largely built-in user metrics. In the past, if a local government were to send out a flyer, the best it could report was the amount of paper printed and possibly a secondary reader percentage. New social and civic media by comparison normally has built-in measurement metrics capabilities. Today, when a local government sends out a message it has the inherent ability to know not only how many people it sent the message to but also whether the message was actually delivered or returned, opened or not, for how long, and how long the recipient spends on a particular page. The PTI survey revealed that a large majority of managers did not use social media metrics because of three stated reasons. They were:

1. They claimed to be too busy and didn't have the time,
2. They claimed that it was too complicated and lacked the proper training,
3. They claimed their supervisors didn't care or never asked.

This is a sharp departure from what one generally finds in the business sector where data is mined every second and decisions are made on having relevant and near-immediate information about people, consumers, trends and habits. Local governments will have a lot of catching up to do in this area.

Apple, who revolutionized the smart phone with the iPhone and surprised even the most critic with the iPad, has enjoyed enormous success with its App Store, where one can browse through over 350,000 apps for the iPhone and over 65,000 apps for the iPad. One can now browse a category appropriately named Government 2.0. Even outside the Apple App Store, apps have been developed by and for local governments that allow citizens to report potholes, animal control issues, graffiti, lighting issues, or to issues involving crimes or accidents, and much more. The new apps allows for pictures to be submitted with the latitude and longitude, exact time, and device owner information. Because apps are usually completely separate from a website, there are greater opportunities for innovation and experimentation.

The Challenge

State and local government leaders and managers are challenged as never before to seek out new and better ways to engage and interact with the publics they serve. With a 97 percent+ penetration rate of mobile devices, which are becoming smarter with each new model, they must understand and adequately address how the publics they serve prefer to be engaged. At the same time, these same managers must always be aware of those in the population who either cannot afford devices and service, or choose to opt out of technology communication solutions. This is referred to as the digital divide or gap. This gap is often misunderstood and some mistakenly believe that the so-called gap refers to poverty as the main cause. Yet there is ample evidence that poverty is but one of many important factors.

Web 2.0 and social or civic media depend on citizens and governments alike to have reliable access to affordable broadband in our homes and offices. The federal regulator of commercial broadband, the Federal Communications Commission (FCC) was charged by Congress to develop a National Broadband Plan for America. After much work, the plan was released to the public in March 2010 and was divided into seven broad categories.

One of the seven major categories is Broadband and Civic Engagement. Here, the report highlighted four key areas, which are:

1. Release more government data online in open and accessible formats to enable the public to more actively participate in the civic life of their communities and their democracy and hold their government accountable.

2. Expand public media's use of digital online platforms and create a 21st century digital national archive to empower people with information on broadband-enabled platforms.

3. Increase opportunities for citizens to participate in the civic life of their local communities and to engage their government through social media and broadband-enabled tools, like smartphones, as well as open platforms and innovative partnerships.

4. Leverage broadband-based technologies to modernize delivery of government services and enhance democratic processes and ensure that they are accessible to all Americans.

While most applaud this report as a significant first step, much (if not all) of the actual recommendations were focused on the federal government and what its agencies should and must do to better engage the public through broadband technology. There is nothing, of course, preventing local governments from adopting many of the key principles, as they (local governments) are after all closest to their citizens – and the good news is they have been doing so long before the report was even begun. Broadband is like electricity in that it is a source or conduit of energy that provides both wired and wireless communications. Web 2.0 and social media depend on reliable broadband to deliver two-way and receive two-way content and information – be it wired or wireless – on a computer, smartphone, or tablet.

Budget woes always bring about new or enhanced forms of innovation. While text is here to stay, video and graphic interfaces have become the new norm. Even before "the Great Recession of 2008-09", advances in technology were making peer-to-peer video conferencing a preferred method for instant meetings. With the advent of improved technologies, there is high definition quality video and sound that is so life-like that people in other locations can't believe they are not in the same room, – hence virtual presence. The next generation of video cameras will be smaller, lighter, and more powerful in every way. New still cameras can take HD video and can easily be connected to the Internet as well as big screen TVs. Citizens will have forward and back facing higher-resolution cameras that will enable greater peer-to-peer and group-to-group communications. Moreover, just as word processing programs allowed almost anyone to be a publisher, new easy-to-use video processor programs allow almost anyone to be a producer of movies.

Moving Forward

This raises many questions regarding the implications for government. The public will expect no less from their government as the private sector is poised to capitalize on the evolving social media revolution. Already the news media is encouraging everyone to be "I reporters" and upload their video clips as stories unfold. Often the first to a scene are amateurs clicking and posting away long before anyone from the media arrives.

Public safety communication officers are beginning to think about new training for their dispatchers who will soon be viewing emergencies from the field in real-time and in HD. They are concerned that many dispatchers may be unprepared for the potential shock of seeing blood and trauma in ways that could be disturbing, shocking, and far more stressful than a phone conversation. So where are we headed and how can governments at all levels best be prepared and respond?

The bottom line here is that blogging, micro-blogging, video posting, picture sharing, are all intricately intertwined and it's not at all unusual for a local government to have multiple sites and or applications that are all linked together to further the virtual and immediate need for connectivity and communication. Adding to this complex maze are the cross boundaries of what is personal and what constitutes professional or business networks. One must also recognize that with all the new social networking technologies, government's technology infrastructure is at greater risk for malicious attacks and breaches in security than ever before.

Despite the concern of threats, thousands of local, state, and federal enterprises are already experimenting with social networks and Web 2.0+ applications. The more challenging for government leaders and managers is determining how it can be best managed and by whom. What follows is a starting point of questions regarding policies and procedures that needs to be explored in just about any governmental organization.

a. What are the jurisdictions' policies toward social networking sites and applications?

b. Who determines (and by what criteria) which websites and applications can be utilized?

c. What safeguards are in place to ensure the highest level of network infrastructure security from all possible malicious threats and intrusions? (Policy, enforcement, and hardware).

d. What process and procedure is in place to monitor certain sites where the public may be participating? This is important to help assess what people are saying and sharing that might be of interest or concern.

e. What process and procedure is in place to thwart any accidental, false, bad, or harmful information? In other words, how are you able to respond to misinformation and mistruths, which in a worst-case scenario create a panic or other harmful response?

f. Moving forward, what will be the role of public access channels that are mostly found on cable? How does this measure up when so many citizens are utilizing web-based technologies?

g. Who is in charge? Are today's web managers equipped with the necessary people skills, training, and management skills to coordinate multiple web-based communication platforms?

h. How does e-government and m-government fit in with a local, state, or federal agency's mission?

i. Who will be the senior person to coordinate all web-centric communications?

j. How will success or failure be measured? There are many "good ideas" floating around in cyber space – but there needs to be a set of metrics where one can periodically assess how the various programs and services are doing.

k. How do the new social media polices impact records retention requirements? How does this impact existing policies and procedures?

l. Are applications for websites and mobile devices optimized for newer technologies such as larger screen devices and tablets?

The cyber world of Web 2.0 and social and civic media is growing rapidly and spreading like a virus. Not all viruses are necessarily bad. It is mutating all the time as new innovators find ways to enhance and build upon the efforts of others. It is a very exciting time to watch this growth – and governments at all levels desperately need to do more than serve as a casual observer. Citizens and their devices will expect nothing less.

CHAPTER 2

Matching Goals to Web 2.0 Tools

Harnessing the Power of Web 2.0 and Social Media

Web 2.0 technologies and civic/social media tools are rapidly transforming the way government is able to interact with citizens and how they manage service delivery. In describing Web 2.0, Gartner uses three anchor points: "a set of technologies with community and social dimensions that enable new business models." While these new technologies and new business models afford opportunities for government to move into the next generation of public service, achieving meaningful results requires a planned approach.

An April 2010 Pew Research Center survey, Government Online,[3] identified that citizens' online "interactions with government are frequently:

- **Data driven** – Efforts by government agencies to post their data online are resonating with citizens. Fully 40 percent of online adults went online in the preceding year to access data and information about government (for instance, by looking up stimulus spending, political campaign contributions or the text of legislation).

- **Organized around new online platforms** – Citizen interactions with government are moving beyond the website. Nearly one third (31 percent) of online adults use online platforms such as blogs, social networking sites, email, online video or text messaging to get government information.

- **Participatory** – Americans are not simply going online for data and information; they want to share their personal views on the business of government. Nearly one quarter (23 percent) of internet users participate in the online debate around government policies or issues, with much of this discussion occurring outside of official government channels."

Like all technology, a Flickr here and a Twitter there does not necessarily harness the potential power that is available through Web 2.0. The use of Web 2.0 and social media should not be just a series of single initiatives; rather it should be a strategic and coordinated way of interacting with citizens and building connected communities. Government leadership will be demonstrated by those organizations that adopt and leverage defined goals for using Web 2.0 tools to take their communications and service delivery to the next level.

The Eight-Step Umbrella

There are eight steps that can help maximize the power of Web 2.0 in a way that goes beyond setting up zippy Facebook pages, although those zippy sites can be a solid and efficient communication channel.

1. Seriously commit to three broad goals for how you use new and emerging technologies. This includes understanding where you are in your use of technology to engage citizens and where you want to be.

2. Learn more about available technologies and invest time in exploring the innovative applications used by other government agencies.

3. Review your technical standards and policies, including electronic communications, privacy, security, accessibility. Have a social media policy. Determine the organizational processes for the use of Web 2.0 and social media.

4. Identify those service areas in which Web 2.0 and social media tools would help to accomplish one or more of the three broad goals for improving citizen participation, government transparency and organizational efficiencies. This may be a problem situation that technologies could help solve.

5. Determine how much communication and interaction you want to have and can support.

6. Establish more specific objectives for your communication/interaction.

7. Select the tool that will work best.

8. Select performance metrics and targets, track performance and adjust.

The Golden Goals for Government

Three broad goals for government use of Web 2.0 and civic/social media are to:

- encourage greater citizen engagement and empowerment
- demonstrate government transparency and accountability
- achieve new operational efficiencies

Achieving these goals is a win-win, as they align citizen expectations of government with government's desired results for service improvements. Web 2.0 technologies and civic media provide channels for greater access, coordination and digital equity. They also move government forward in the use of more efficient and flexible technologies, such as centralized data warehouses, real-time and self-service interactions, multi-channel and multi-media communications, and location-based services.

Citizen Engagement – Mostly, the focus of government is on internal priorities and solutions. Efforts for citizen participation typically have been part of a required check-off before big projects are initiated or an annual satisfaction survey. Accountability typically has been the Performance Report section of the annual budget.

A significant limitation has been access, with input offered from small groups of the same individuals who regularly comment at meetings and attend town hall meetings. Web applications, especially new media, dramatically changed the access parameters. Citizens can interact with government 24x7, with choices for preferred channel of communication. Governments can distribute real-time information to the general public or to targeted groups. Information can quickly go "viral" to reach millions of people.

Citizens want to use the same tools they are using to connect and share with family and friends, and to bank, buy and browse. Governments are responding. As shown in Figure 2 (see page 14) featuring a tool used by the City of Fort Collins, Colorado,[4] a very common Web 2.0 application which could be found this past year on state and local government websites is a "Budget Calculator," an interactive dashboard for residents to prioritize the funding of services.

Transparency and Accountability – Public trust in government is a universal issue. Across the country, citizens have voiced their expectations for government accountability, especially in areas such as financial management. At the same time, governments recognize that trust is a key factor in gaining citizen support for important programs and projects. Web 2.0 technologies provide a multitude of ways to enable citizens to access relevant data, from progress on bond projects to neighborhood crime reports.

Governments should consider the target groups for their communications. For example, a notable distinction to make for financial reports is that auditors and tax-concerned groups may be comfortable with 30-page spreadsheets, but most residents would rather view summary data, photos of results and maps or zip code searches to localize information for their neighborhoods.

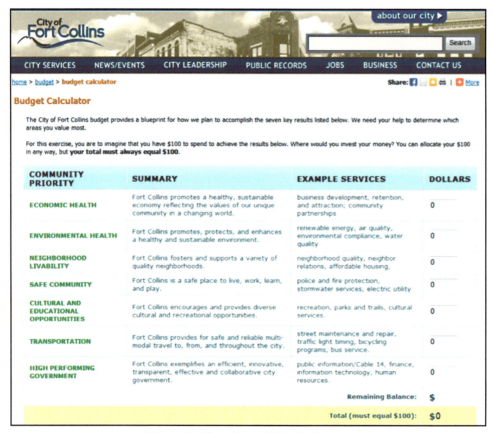

Figure 2. City of Fort Collins, Colorado

Many governments have centralized knowledge bases, CRMs, work management systems, and interfaced enterprise systems to support their customer contact center operations, web-based services, asset management and performance reporting. As system providers have become less proprietary, governments have moved to open source systems, and new mobile application developers are joining the market, integrating data from existing systems with Web 2.0 applications and social media is becoming less challenging. In fact, many enterprise systems now include applications for Web 2.0, social media and mobile.

Pinellas County, Florida, holds "eTown Halls," which are live, interactive forums that enable citizens to discuss specific topics with a panel comprised of their government officials and subject matter experts.

The application leverages Facebook, YouTube, Twitter, Cover-It Live, QR codes, subscription service, tele-town hall and an associated web survey.

They have about 1,000 participants per eTown Hall, compared to an average of 100 participants at a traditional town hall venue. Recent topics include Budget 2011-2012, Volunteers in Pinellas, Transportation and Hurricanes: Surviving the Storm. Program archives are accessible, as shown in Figure 3.[5]

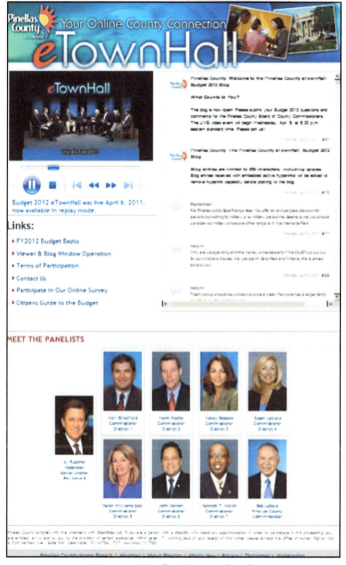

Figure 3. Pinellas County, Florida

Improved Efficiencies – The country's severe economic and financial crisis has profoundly impacted state and local government budgets, accentuating the proverbial call for governments to provide better public services with fewer resources. Web 2.0 and social media help governments to work toward greater efficiencies. Research by both Gartner and Forrester indicates that offloading citizen calls to a self-service web channel can generate savings of at least $4.00 per contact. Web 2.0 and social media can provide additional cost savings through streamlined processes, shared and coordinated data access, and embedded mapping, as well as reduced requirements for time, travel and staffing.

MyGovIdea/IdeaMachine, shown in Figure 4,[6] is an ongoing eDemocracy effort to continuously collect and evaluate ideas that could save money, improve service or create efficiencies throughout Miami-Dade County government. The initial launch, known as the "Idea Machine," was targeted to county employees, enabled by discussion forum and workflow technology and implemented on the county's employee portal. In 2010, the application was made available as MyGovIdea to citizens through Miamidade.gov.

Since inception of the project, Miami-Dade County has received more than 2,100 ideas, with more than 36,000 votes cast. Residents and employees have submitted more than 900 comments about the ideas. County departments reported first-year cost savings of almost $1.2 million as a result of implementing 85 ideas. The tool is fully integrated with miamidade.gov's content management system, enabling widespread usage throughout the county. The application is available on Miami Dade County's ShareGov site to other municipalities who want to implement the system/technology. MyGovIdea does not use any proprietary frameworks, making it readily interoperable with other systems (see Figure 4, page 17).

Where Are You In Citizen Engagement?

As you look to implement Web 2.0 technologies, consider where you are as an organization and where you want to be (see Figure 5, page 17).

Matching Goals to Web 2.0 and Social Media Tools

As you identify specific focus areas for improved communications and engagement, determine what level of interactions you want to accomplish through the use of Web 2.0 and social media.

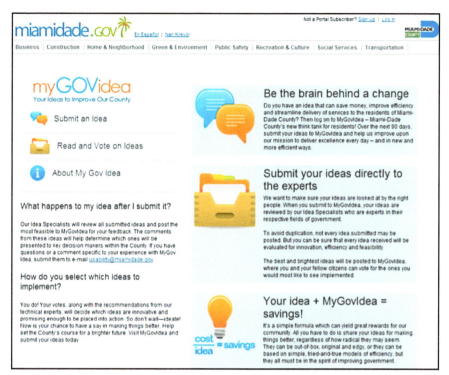

Figure 4. Miami-Dade County, Florida

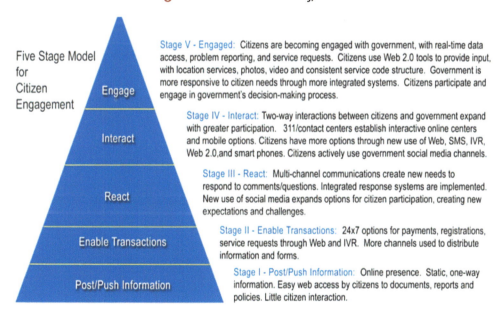

Five Stage Model for Citizen Engagement

Stage V - Engaged: Citizens are becoming engaged with government, with real-time data access, problem reporting, and service requests. Citizens use Web 2.0 tools to provide input, with location services, photos, video and consistent service code structure. Government is more responsive to citizen needs through more integrated systems. Citizens participate and engage in government's decision-making process.

Stage IV - Interact: Two-way interactions between citizens and government expand with greater participation. 311/contact centers establish interactive online centers and mobile options. Citizens have more options through new use of Web, SMS, IVR, Web 2.0,and smart phones. Citizens actively use government social media channels.

Stage III - React: Multi-channel communications create new needs to respond to comments/questions. Integrated response systems are implemented. New use of social media expands options for citizen participation, creating new expectations and challenges.

Stage II - Enable Transactions: 24x7 options for payments, registrations, service requests through Web and IVR. More channels used to distribute information and forms.

Stage I - Post/Push Information: Online presence. Static, one-way information. Easy web access by citizens to documents, reports and policies. Little citizen interaction.

Figure 5. Five Stage Model for Citizen Engagement[7]

Communication & Interaction

▶ Push Information – news, announcements, project updates, meeting notices, traffic/construction notices, education, alerts, updates

▶ Lead back to website and specific applications, creating cross-website synergy

▶ Enable comments/questions – opinions, requests for information or service

▶ Be responsive
   • by linking to service request system
   • by call agent email or live call
   • by posting on application page
   • by live text chat
   • by integrated service request system and tracking number

▶ Drive discussions – broader feedback

▶ Enable active participation in content, including multi-media

Examples:

▶ **Offloading call center agent calls for information** to self-service

▶ **Expanded promotion** of events, meetings and registration processes, such as youth sports leagues, town hall meetings, immunizations, senior programs

▶ **Centralized communications for media** access to replace multiple news releases

▶ **Alerts and updates for weather and emergencies**, with crowd-sourcing participation using photos, video and location mapping

▶ Communication **campaigns for new or changed services**, allowing comments/questions and follow-up for areas of confusion

▶ Easy **access to neighborhood specific information**, such as crime data, location of service crews (e.g. garbage, recycling, mosquito spraying, graffiti removal) through mapping or zip code searches

▶ **Self-service problem reporting**, through which a citizen can report graffiti, potholes, abandoned car, attach a photo and submit through an online service center or a mobile application, all integrated with the 311/call center service request system

While declaring generic, lofty goals may be an easy task, a number of challenges exist for government implementation of Web 2.0 technologies and tools:

- Identifying focus areas and making wise choices about the right tools
- Understanding that it takes more than dedicated staff and that there will be increased decision-making cycle time and response time
- Dealing with the rapid growth of technology that makes training a challenge
- Addressing the tendency to rush to get technologies adopted, and then focusing on getting more users and more content, rather than better content focused on mission
- Helping leaders and staff recognize the potential benefits of interactive information-sharing systems
- Getting over the fear of mixed messages, rumors, and perceived loss of control
- Establishing policies that outline expectations, standards and processes for information-sharing, interaction levels, coordination, and content
- Overcoming resource limitations, such as staffing, cost of interfaces, changing technology, and obstacles such as security, bandwidth, employee productivity, coordination and Freedom of Information Act issues
- Ensuring quality, accuracy and consistency of information
- Coordinating information and applications across departments and agencies

Government use of social media goes beyond socializing, and construction of social media tools is measurably different for public organizations than for individuals and the private sector.

The Web 2.0 Tools

While there is no set definition for Web 2.0, it can be described as interactive, social, dynamic, user-centered, collaborative and interoperable. Some of the tools are social networks, wikis, mashups, RSS feeds, listservs, alerts, blogs and microblogs, mapping, dynamic input and service requests, photo sharing, webcasts and webcams, video sharing, podcasts and vodcasts, virtual worlds, games and search engine utilities.

Social Networks

There are a number of social networks out there – Wikipedia lists 177 major sites – but **Facebook** is the key platform with the majority of users. Other examples include Yelp,

Bebo, MySpace, LinkedIn, Friendster, Ning, Nexo, Classmates, Habbo (teens), My Life, MyHeritage, Study VZ, and Tagged.

Some Stats

▶ Percent of online adults (18+) using social media: 65 percent.

▶ 90 percent of Internet users know at least one social network.

▶ The average social user has 195 friends.

▶ Social networking site usage grew 88 percent among Internet users aged 55-64 between April 2009 and May 2010.

Facebook

Facebook communications have high value for government, as it is fast, friendly and includes many features, like automatic posting to Twitter, content sharing for photos and video, blog imports, built-in RSS feed, mobile options and usage data and charts. Facebook provides setting options for flexibility to use only to push information or encourage active outside participation.

Some Stats

▶ During the average 20-minute period in 2010, there were 1,587,000 wall posts, 2,716,000 photos uploaded and 10,208,000 comments posted on Facebook.

▶ The average Facebook user is connected to 60 pages, groups and events.

▶ Average time spent each month on Facebook.com per user is 4 hours 35 minutes.

Many cities, counties and states have a general Facebook site, and some have specific service area sites, such as for an airports, parks or emergency management. As reflected in Figure 6,[8] the City of Chesapeake, Virginia has a great Facebook success story.

In Chesapeake, Virginia, arsonists torched the Fun Forest playground in Chesapeake City Park. The Fun Forest Facebook page was built to raise awareness and money to rebuild the burned section of the park. The Facebook page generated widespread community participation, with over 5,000 "likers," donations for the rebuild $87,767, and 1,800 volunteers donated a total of 21,600 hours over two weekends in winter weather. The project also received a donation from Sears, valued at $30,000, and a community with a vested interest in the park (see Figure 6, page 21).

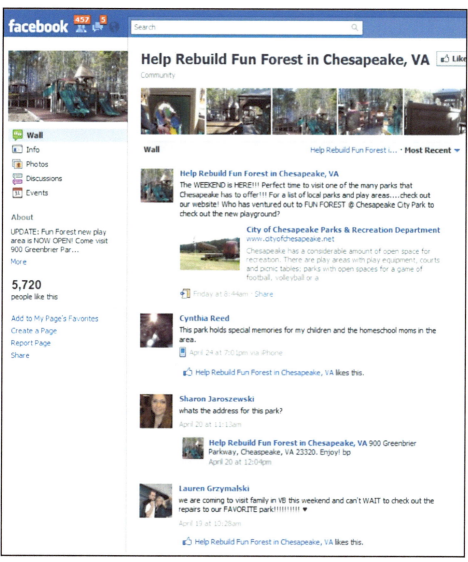

Figure 6. City of Chesapeake, Virginia

One observation about government Facebook sites is that those that only push information do not have as many regular viewers as those who allow comments, questions and
discussions. A dynamic Facebook page requires frequent and interesting posts, active
citizen participation and timely responses to questions. Pushing information works best
on microblogs with links back to a website.

Blogs/Microblogs

A blog (a contraction of the term "web log") is a type of website, usually maintained by an individual with regular entries of commentary, descriptions of events, or other material such as graphics or video. Entries are commonly displayed in reverse-chronological order. Blogs can be as long as needed. A microblog is another type of blog, featuring very short posts.

The major blog platforms are WordPress and Tumblr. WordPress.com is an open source, hosted blog and is known for its ease of use. WordPress.org provides open source, downloadable software to install on your own server and has a lot of functionality. WordPress.com has millions of blog sites and viewers and provides different levels of ease and options for photos and video, with some functions requiring plug-ins or purchased upgrades. Tumblr has over 15 million blogs, gets millions of daily posts and is getting billions of page views per day globally. It allows you to post text, photos, links, video, slideshows, has options to customize, interfaces with YouTube, Twitter, Facebook, and the ability to "reblog."

Blogs work best when focused on a specific topic or area of interest, such as a museum program, green initiatives or a mayor's communication tool. The State of California actively uses blogs, and one developed in WordPress by the Department of Fish and Game is shown in Figure 7.[9] A caution for government organizations is that broad, public blogs must be closely monitored. In a 2010 PTI survey, a number of cities and counties indicated they had stopped a blog because of poor participation and the lack of perceived value (see Figure 7, page 23).

Twitter

A microblog differs from a traditional blog in that its content is typically smaller. In addition to hosted platforms, free and open source software is available for organizations to set up their own microblogging service for collaborative or informal communications among work groups. The most popular and widely used microblog is Twitter, which limits postings to 140 characters. A key value of Twitter is the speed in posting and in citizen access to information. Twitter can appreciably extend the reach of communications as followers retweet posts to existing community networks. It is great for pushing information, such as fast, centralized communications with news media and for weather and traffic alerts. New third-party apps, plug-ins and customizations are becoming available all the time.

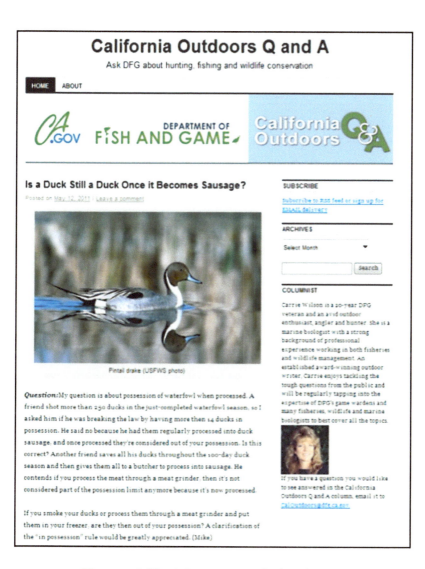

Figure 7. California Department of Fish and Game

Some Stats

▶ Twitter's Web platform only accounts for a quarter of its users – 75 percent use third-party applications.

▶ Twitter gets more than 300,000 new users every day.

▶ There are currently 110 million users of Twitter's services.

▶ Twitter receives 180 million unique visits each month.

- There are more than 600 million searches on Twitter every day.
- From April 2010 to April 2011, Twitter has gained 40 million users and a 62 percent increase in mobile use of the platform.
- Average time spent each month on Twitter.com per user is 2 hours 12 minutes.

The State of Utah has utilized Twitter, along with other Web 2.0 tools, to improve communication with the media and ultimately the public. Their Department of Public Safety (DPS) developed a centralized Media Portal, which is available online and through mobile phones. The portal integrates active incident feed, news stories and pushed alerts. They use Twitter, as displayed in Figure 8,[10] to notify the media and general public about current issues and incidents, and provide real-time access to reporters, with a secure login, to dispatch calls and multimedia files. The most relevant incidences are displayed to the media based on geographic location utilizing HTML5. With over 400 active users consisting of news directors, reporters, and interagency monitors representing 100 percent of all major media outlets in Utah, the application has proven extremely effective and has improved public safety throughout the state of Utah. With active media and public Twitter followers, call volume has dropped by over 40 percent during high-profile incidents.

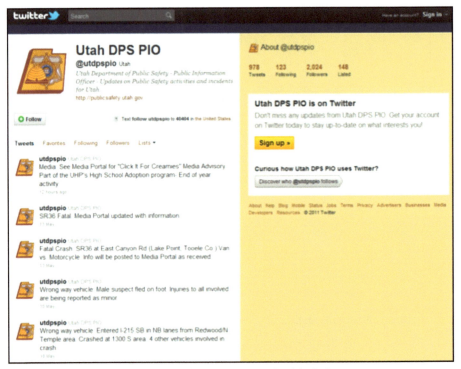

Figure 8. Utah Department of Public Safety

A discussion of government use of Twitter should include a reference to Cory Booker, mayor of Newark, New Jersey, who received national attention for his active and responsive use of Twitter during the 2010 snowstorms. As shown in Figure 9,[11] Mayor Booker continues to use the platform, with a following of over one million people.

Figure 9. Mayor Cory Booker, Newark, New Jersey

Social Content Sharing

Social content sharing includes photos, video and podcasts. The key platforms are Flickr for photos and YouTube for video. The most widely used format for podcasts is MP3.

For government, video is useful for meeting and event records; for educational efforts, such as explaining processes for code enforcement, new recycling programs and pollution prevention; for public service announcements; and for crime prevention programs like Crime Stoppers.

Excellent uses for photo sharing include spotlighting unique attributes of your community, the work of local artists or community initiatives like neighborhood clean-ups.

Governments also can use applications that enable citizens to upload and share photos of graffiti and potholes, or specific site conditions during an emergency. Photos can be a high impact way to provide before and after updates to citizens on bond program progress or a visual of how CDBG or grant funds were used, instead of typical spreadsheets or large volume reports.

Podcasts can be useful for a Mayor's state of the city address or for tours of local museum exhibits.

Some platforms for social content sharing have limits or standards for size, length and formats. For example, the Facebook limit on video is 20 minutes and 1 GB, while You-Tube's limit is 15 minutes and 2 GB. They both will extend these limits in some cases. An important thing to remember is your audience, and knowing if citizens in your community will download and listen to a podcast that isn't music-related. According to the PEW Research Center, podcast downloading continues to increase, but podcasts have yet to become a fixture in the everyday lives of Internet users.[12]

Just as technology is transforming rapidly, social media changes on a regular basis, with expanded options and new functionality. For example, Twitter recently partnered with Flickr, YouTube and other social media providers for linkage and embedded photos and videos. New features are getting cooler, but a key to the effectiveness and efficiencies of social media for government is finding functionality that accomplishes your goals and, on a practical level, is easy to maintain and update. If the staff with responsibility leaves, the next person should be able to easily pick it up.

Web 2.0 and social media enabled Fairfax County, Virginia to move from distributing public and targeted communications through over 20 different department websites to a centralized multi-media news center called "Newswire." As viewed in Figure 10,[13] the one-stop news shop functions as an umbrella for many related tools and interactivity. including RSS feeds for selected topics; publishing to Twitter, Facebook, YouTube and Flickr; event maps; social voting and a discussion forum called "Ask Fairfax!" (see Figure 10, page 27).

 Wikis

A wiki is a website that is developed and updated collaboratively through the work of multiple authors. Wikis can be open for anyone to view and make changes, or they can be viewable to the public, with editing restricted to members. A wiki also can be closed so that only community members can both view and edit content.

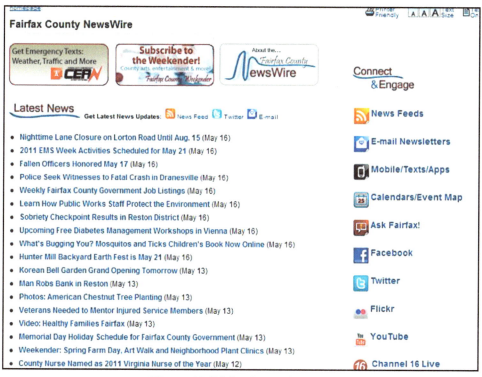

Figure 10. Fairfax County, Virginia

There are over 100 wiki platforms or options, mostly open source, some hosted free or for ads or monthly fees and some downloads to your own server. The most popular Wiki software package is MediaWiki, which is free and open source, and is what was used to create Wikipedia, the most well-known public wiki. You can view and compare wiki software packages at a site called Wikimatrix.

Wikis are very efficient communication and coordination tools. They work well in government for internal department/agency work groups, project management, information sharing among specific public groups with common interest (arts, libraries) and interagency collaboration and knowledge sharing (technology, education, public safety and emergency management). The tool has been used actively and successfully at the federal level by the State Department, the CIA, the Pentagon and the Office of the Director of National Intelligence. Two years after launching in 2006, the State Department's Diplopedia had over 3,700 articles, 700 registered editors and half-million page views. The City of Arvada, Colorado's content management system, which controls all content on its websites, works as a closed wiki, with all authenticated users having the ability to contribute.

Additionally, their intranet uses this technology for internal documentation. Not many public wikis currently are being utilized by state and local governments.

A key to effective use of a wiki internally or cross-agency is to have defined participation and editing roles, so that each contributor adds to the focus area or has an area of responsibility or section to provide current information and updates so that a more complete and useful knowledge base is developed and available to everyone involved.

Mashups and Mapping

A mashup is a web page or application that blends (or mashes) together data, presentation or functionality from two or more sources or feeds into a new integrated service. Primary characteristics of a mashup are combination, visualization and aggregation.

The New York City Department of Transportation leverages social media and mobile applications to address communities of interest around certain traffic and travel topics, and to improve service delivery to the public. Using mashups of data from transportation studies, blogs on potholes, iPhone applications to promote safe driving, and more, the Department of Transportation provides easy to access and relevant information to citizens. As shown in Figure 11,[14] the mashup of the Jackson Heights Neighborhood Transportation Study, which includes data-driven recommendations, data map and RSS feed, is automatically set to display traffic speeds on weekdays, with options for turning on and off different data layers, such as pedestrian volumes and crashes (see Figure 11, page 29).

Dynamic Input and Service Requests

A number of state and local governments now have integrated online service request systems. The City and County of Denver's 311 Online Call Center, shown in Figure 12[15] (see page 30), provides two-way interaction and includes their 311 call center, as well as 16 agencies throughout the City and County of Denver that are managing customer service cases initiated by the call center through their CRM application. Their goal is to reduce call volumes and increase citizen accessibility to request services by driving citizens to the website, a lower cost channel. Denver created a web service interface between its CRM system and denvergov.org website, which is brokered by an enterprise service bus (ESB) in an SOA suite. It allows for a real time, flexible, extensible tool that includes configuration hosted on the ESB. This architecture enables a CRM search for existing customers before creating new ones, immediate delivery of CRM case numbers to citizens who create an online case, the ability for citizens to attach documents and photos to cases, with storage in a document management system. In 2010, Denver received 29,000 online case submissions and estimate approximately 35,000 online cases

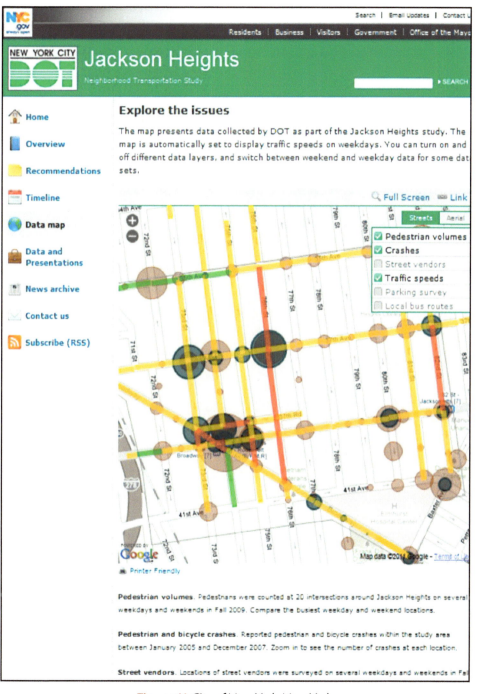

Figure 11. City of New York, New York

in 2011. They have completed an iPhone application, which will be available soon. The 311 online request system was developed via a web service framework to allow for extensibility, data sharing, and re-use.

Figure 12. City and County of Denver, Colorado

Subscription Services for Web Page Updates and News

Subscription Services enable citizens to sign up to receive notifications of new postings on web pages and news updates. Subscribers often can choose the type/topic and the delivery channel, such as email or SMS. Subscriptions.IN.gov is an online, e-subscription management service for the State of Indiana. Website visitors can subscribe to e-mail and wireless updates for specific content on agency sites. The service is offered free to all state agencies, so they can leverage the tool at no cost and allow their end users to become active participants in government by keeping them abreast of the latest developments. Since its inception, Subscriptions.IN.gov has gained a following of 851,904 subscribers. Of these subscribers, there are a total of 1,410,431 subscriptions to the individual topics available. A total of 2,790,518 bulletins have been sent to the individual topic subscriptions. The bulletins have been viewed 201,793,180 times and account for 5,987,768 visits to the IN.gov Portal. Over

73 State entities are currently utilizing the tool to communicate with their constituents. As shown in Figure 13,[16] the enterprise implementation allows IN.gov to offer over 1,500 subscription topics. All of the email subscriptions and user preferences are stored in a single location and are accessible from the admin interface. Several State agencies are beginning to utilize the tool in unique ways. The Indiana Board of Animal Health has added an email subscription to its newsroom RSS feed, which is populated by the State-wide Press Release tool. The Indiana Department of Environmental Management has added the subscription service to a mobile application developed by Indiana Interactive, which displays the water quality at certain Indiana beaches.

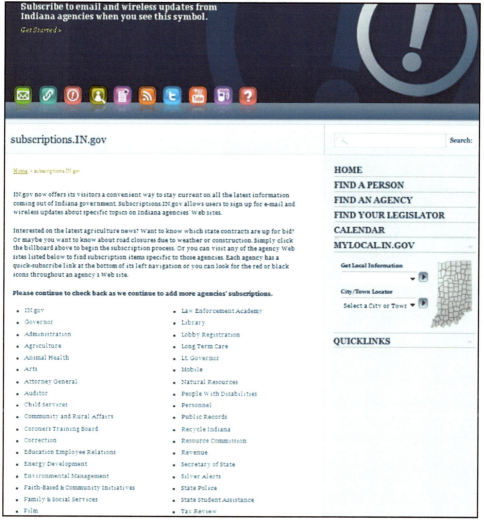

Figure 13. State of Indiana

Notify Me focuses on current and potential residents and business owners of Richland, Washington and the surrounding area to receive instant notifications and information from various city departments about programs and activities. By receiving the information at the first of the week, citizens have a reminder – or first notice – about meetings they want to attend or volunteer position for which they may apply. Shown in Figure 14,[17] Notify Me is integrated with the city's service request system and with the City's online Bid Posting, News Flash and Calendar services. Notify Me information is provided in text and email messages that can reach subscribers through personal computers and mobile phones.

Figure 14. Richland, Washington

Alerts

Some citizens prefer to have a separate notification process for emergency type situations, using other social media tools for news and information. Montgomery County uses the Roam Secure Alert Network to contact subscribers during a major crisis, emergency, or severe weather event. Residents may register for optional groups, or for only the most urgent alerts (e.g. water main break, tornado warning). As described in Figure 15,[18] Alert Montgomery delivers important emergency alerts, notifications and updates through multiple devices at the same time, including email, cell phone, text pager, BlackBerry, wireless PDA, XM Radio Channel, Twitter and Facebook. Alert Montgomery now exceeds 113,000 accounts and 201,496 subscribed devices receiving alerts.

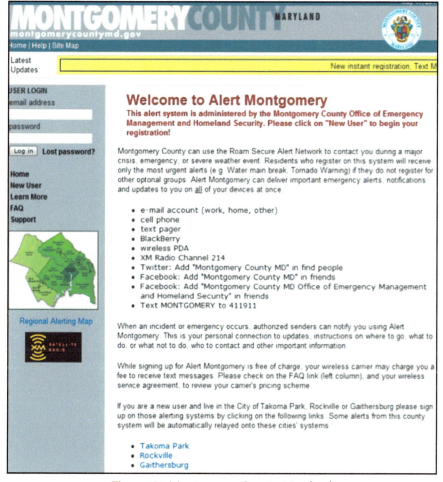

Figure 15. Montgomery County, Maryland

Live Online Chat

Chat is like instant messaging on a website. The State of Texas's "Get Satisfaction" application, seen in Figure 16,[19] is an interactive online resource available on two areas of the Texas.gov website. The Ask section (www.texas.gov/ask) provides direct communications with customer support representatives and the Connect section (www.texas.gov/connect) is a collaborative forum for Texans to engage with each other by sharing ideas, comments, feedback, and more. Get Satisfaction, shown in Figure 15, is a powerful Web 2.0 platform for crowdsourced customer service and information sharing among users. The Get Satisfaction forum is integrated with Texas.gov customer support and call center processes. The Texas.gov customer support team provides the majority of responses to all forum posts. Currently, 27 percent of Texas.gov Get Satisfaction visitors have participated in the customer support forum by posting a support topic or question. To date, the Texas.gov Get Satisfaction site has received 11,362 visits, with 416 visitors posting support topics/questions.

Figure 16. State of Texas

Mobile Applications

Mobile technologies afford government significant opportunities for achieving greater cost optimization, improved communications and data coordination, expanded service delivery and much progress towards digital equality. They offer wider reach, more personalization for targeting, cost-effectiveness, faster information flow, and better management. Mobile technologies are empowering citizens in all aspects of their daily lives. More people can afford a mobile phone than a personal computer and are comfortable learning to use mobile devices. The popularity of social media and use of Web 2.0 tools also is transferring easily to mobile applications. The prevalent use of mobile phones by citizens provides a communication channel that vastly improves the time and ease in which citizens can access and interact with government.

Some Stats

▶ Over 2 million units of Microsoft's Windows Phone 7 operating system were shipped in the final quarter of 2010.

▶ 16.24 million Apple iPhones were sold worldwide by the end of 2010.

▶ There are more than 100 million active users currently accessing Facebook through their mobile devices.

▶ More than a third of users access Twitter via their mobile phone.

▶ The number of text messages sent and received everyday exceeds the population of the planet. Ninety-three percent of all adults own a cell phone.

The City of Corpus Christi's mobile application for citizens, CCMobile, shown in Figure 17[20] (see page 36), enables residents to download a free application to use their smart phones to quickly photograph issues, select a service category from a dropdown menu (e.g. pothole, graffiti, junk vehicle) and hit the send button for real-time problem reporting. The service request, with physical address via GPS coordinates and date/time stamp, goes into the City's online service request system and is processed by a Customer Service Center call agent. In the first month of deployment, CCMobile had over 1,500 downloads on Blackberry, iPhone and Android phones with 94 service requests. Seven months later, the application had been downloaded over 2,500 times, with over 400 service requests submitted. The majority of issues related to heavy brush, illegal dumping, stray animals, premise violations and high grass. The integrated systems enable citizens to submit service requests via smartphones or online using the same platform, backend systems and knowledge base. In addition, on the same CCMobile website, you can use map markers on an interactive map to view specific problems reported, with photos,

Figure 17. City of Corpus Christi, Texas

addresses, service request numbers, and status. You also can vote, view other reports in the same neighborhood or leave a comment.

The City of Menifee, California, also has an integrated and multi-channel citizen engagement tool. Their Citizen Request Tracker, shown in Figure 18,[21] allows residents to submit requests and concerns to the City 24 hours a day from their computer or iPhone and monitor the progress of the request once it's submitted. The CRT system also improves workflow by streamlining the requests and routing them to pre-determined staff members.

Figure 18. Menifee, California

The City of Santa Monica, California, has a very targeted and economically beneficial mobile application, seen in Figure 19 [22] (see page 38). The City provides real-time parking availability information in the form of an XML feed. The XML data represents the location and number of available parking spaces in both the downtown district and beaches. Automobile traffic entering and exiting downtown structures and beach lots is measured using pavement sensors and transmitted via fiber optic communication lines to the city parking office. The data is currently used in a Google provided maplet (desktop and mobile) as well as in a third-party mobile application. This tool is completely integrated with the City's centralized parking management system. Access to parking information helps stimulate economic growth as residents and visitors have advance information and directions to the best parking options, thus spending more time, in a better mood, enjoying entertainment, shopping and dining, as well as the pier and beaches.

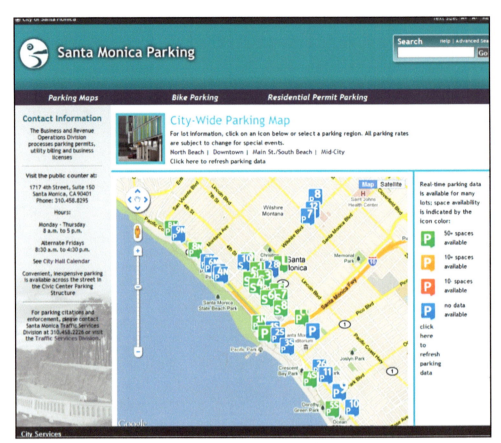

Figure 19. Santa Monica, California

RSS Feeds

RSS is a means by which frequently updated Web content from a variety of sources, such as news headlines or blog entries, can be aggregated and displayed on a single page by a Web browser or email reader. RSS feeds allow people to easily retrieve the latest content from the websites they like. It saves time because you do not need to visit each site individually to see if there is new information or subscribe to each site's email newsletter. Individuals use a Feed Reader or News Aggregator that grabs their selected feeds from various sites. The most popular feed readers are Google Reader and MyYahoo. Most social media and many CRM and other systems and applications now include RSS capability. Several good examples of services that help webmasters manage their RSS feed updates are Feedburner and Technorati.

QR Codes

A QR code (Quick Response or Reference), a type of mobile tag, is a matrix barcode readable by QR barcode readers and camera phones. The code has black modules in a square pattern on a white background. QR codes are more functional than standard bar codes, as they can store and digitally present more data, including URL links, geographic coordinates and text. Most new smartphones already have QR code readers and they are also readily available, as are sites for easily generating codes.

A number of local and state governments are utilizing QR codes in their citizen engagement efforts. Pinellas County has bar code communications for emergency management and hurricane information, including evacuation routes, court assistance, and sign-up for social media updates. They even have video that explains how the QR codes work. New York City uses QR codes on the side of garbage trucks for videos about recycling and have launched an initiative to put QR codes on all building permits by 2013, enabling individuals to have easy access to information about buildings, construction sites, approved scope of work, the site manager and other project details.

A Great Example of Web 2.0 Strategies and Goals

In their Spring 2011 ROAD MAP FOR THE DIGITAL CITY, Achieving New York City's Digital Future,[23] the City of New York maps their goals for Web 2.0 and social media:

Characteristics of effective public service social media:

1. Provides clear value to the user. Answers the question: Why would a citizen want to use this? What do they gain?
2. Citizen-centric, not agency-centric. Communicates on the terms of the individual.
3. Agency social media managers actively contribute, supporting a dynamic community.
4. Aligns with agency goals, improving the City's ability to serve New Yorkers and ensuring adequate resource commitment.

Engagement

The City will improve digital tools including nyc.gov and 311 online to streamline service and enable citizen-centric, collaborative government. It will expand social media engagement, implement new internal coordination measures, and continue to solicit community input in the following ways:

1. Relaunch nyc.gov to make the City's website more usable, accessible, and intuitive
2. Expand 311 Online through smartphone apps, Twitter and live chat
3. Implement a custom bit.ly url redirection service on nyc.gov to encourage sharing and transparency
4. Launch official Facebook presence to engage New Yorkers and customize experience
5. Launch @nycgov, a central Twitter account and one-stop shop of crucial news and services
6. Launch a New York City Tumblr vertical, featuring content and commentary on City stories
7. Launch a Foursquare badge that encourages use of New York City's free public places
8. Integrate crowdsourcing tools for emergency situations
9. Introduce digital Citizen Toolkits for engaging with New York City government online
10. Introduce smart, a team of the City's social media leaders
11. Host New York City's first hackathon: Reinventing nyc.gov
12. Launch an ongoing listening sessions across the five boroughs to encourage input

The State of New York provides advocacy, coordination and support to state agencies through their online, one-stop shop for Web 2.0 information, tools and resources, shown in Figure 20.[24] The Empire 2.0 Center for Excellence encourages New York State agencies to embrace Web 2.0 technologies to more effectively interact with citizens, businesses, employees and visitors with increased efficiency, collaboration, transparency, and openness. It provides methods to help meet the ongoing challenge in providing excellent citizen service and secure access to important information, while reducing costs, risks, and technical complexity. The Empire 2.0 Center for Excellence features:

▶ A "Resources Section" with step-by-step guidance on implementing Web 2.0 technologies, tool kits to help plan and create a social media technology strategy and web pages;

▶ An "Interactive Forum Section" to participate in informal conversations to engage with other social media technology users in open and engaging dialogues about Web 2.0 technologies. Here you can post questions and offer suggestions;

- A "Blog Section" maintained by CIO/OFT with cutting-edge information on social media technology activities and happenings across the state enterprise, around the nation, and even around the globe.

- A "Calendar of Events" to keep you informed on upcoming social media events.

- A "Repository of Articles" to give you one place to access information on the most cutting-edge industry and government practices in social media technologies.

Fifty-three state agencies now using social networking technologies. Twenty New York State agencies are currently using Facebook, 19 state agencies are using Twitter, and 16 state agencies have a YouTube page. In addition, many state agencies use Wikis and blogs.

Figure 20. State of New York

Moving Forward

By determining communication and citizen participation goals, focusing on areas for government accountability and identifying opportunities for operational efficiencies, governments can more effectively review, select and maximize the value of Web 2.0 technologies and move to new levels of performance, citizen engagement and connectivity.

CHAPTER 3

Key Considerations for Public Officials and Staff

Once a desired result for Web 2.0 and social media is defined, a target audience is identified, goals are set and best Web 2.0 tools are identified, processes for implementation and management need to be developed and clearly understood. Several key issues and potential challenges should be considered by public officials and staff, including policies, standards, legal requirements and resource allocations.

Social implies interaction and media implies communication of data. Some people might just think of social network tools like Facebook or Twitter when talking about social media. Web 2.0 is a broader term that includes those and other tools such as mashups, mapping and mobile applications. A good social media policy should apply to all technology tools that are interactive, dynamic, user-centered, collaborative, and interoperable. In addition, a social media policy should be complemented by technical standards and privacy and accessibility policies. Having an effective framework and guide can minimize obstacles and problems related to Web 2.0 and social media applications.

The Social Media Policy – An Outline of Possibilities

Lead cities, counties and states include some or most of these items in their social media policies, emphasizing those areas relevant to their jurisdictions and processes. Some also include individual procedures for different types of social media, such as Facebook, Twitter, and blogs. Some have separate documents for tool guides. Examples of current policies are provided in Chapter 5 and over 20 policies from cities, counties and states are accessible online for PTI members at www.pti.org.

1. Purpose of social media
2. Purpose of policy
3. Somewhere there is a list of definitions for social media tools
4. Some include responsibility as a major category
5. Some include administration, ownership, identification and monitoring

6. Policy
   a. Who represents the government and how the government is represented
   b. Following established laws and policies
      i. Copyright
      ii. Records Retention Requirements
      iii. Public Information Act
      iv. First Amendment of the U.S. Constitution
      v. Privacy Laws
      vi. Information Security Policies
      vii. Freedom of Information Act (FOIA) and ediscovery laws
   c. Right to restrict or remove
      i. Comments not topically related to the particular social medium article being commented upon
      ii. Comments in support of or opposition to political campaigns or ballot measures
      iii. Profane language or content
      iv. Content that contains obscenity (or material that appeals to the prurient interest)
      v. Content that promotes, fosters, or perpetuates discrimination on the basis of race, creed, color, age, religion, gender, marital status, status with regard to public assistance, national origin, physical or mental disability or sexual orientation
      vi. Solicitations of commerce (or advertises or promotes a commercial product or service, or any entity or individual)
      vii. Conduct or encouragement of illegal activity or incites or promotes violence or illegal activities
      viii. Information that may tend to compromise the safety or security of the public or public systems
      ix. Content that violates a legal ownership interest of any other party
      x. Contains personal identifying information or sensitive personal information, as defined in (state code)
   d. Applicable government security policies

e. Required content

    i. Statement that everything is subject to public disclosure

    ii. Must direct back to official website for more information, documents, forms, services necessary to conduct business of government

    iii. Government contact information

    iv. Disclaimer for add-on content out of government control

7. Process

  a. Training requirement

  b. Approval procedures

  c. Addressing customer complaints or service requests

  d. Content, messaging and dialogue

  e. Factual, accurate and timely response

  f. Understanding of widely accessible, not retractable content

  g. Postings based on area of expertise

  h. Consistency with other content provided through other media

  i. Minimum need of weekly updates (or definition of what constitutes need)

  j. Electronic marketing and outreach

  k. Style and branding

  l. Linking

8. Employee Participation in Social Networking (or User Guidelines – may be a separate document)

  a. Reference to government policies (e.g. electronic communications)

  b. Official government business use

  c. Limited personal use (with examples)

  d. Restrictions from personal use

    i. Content posting and sharing

    ii. Personal or financial gain

    iii. Discourteous

    iv. Solicitation

    v. Jokes

<ol type="i" start="6">
<li>Discrimination</li>
<li>Pornography, hate group or gambling</li>
</ol>

<ol type="a" start="5">
<li>Disclosure of confidential information</li>
<li>Authorization process</li>
<li>Privacy</li>
<li>Government representation</li>
</ol>

9. Discipline up to termination statement

It is important for government managers to define standards and provide guidance for the structure, content and processes for their social media sites, not only for public use but also for staff use. Governments need to ensure that laws and ordinances are followed. Often, government leaders are not aware of the number and format of many "official" social media sites developed and managed by department or agency staff. Sometimes, the staff person who is responsible for the Facebook or Twitter site does not know public records or other requirements. In one case, a departmental Facebook page was set up for an individual rather than an organization, and the profile page included personal information, as well as a link to person's side business and to business pages of friends. Clearly communicated policies and standards can minimize these types of issues.

Social Media Liability and Governing Laws

Some policies address terms of service for social media platforms, specifically issues related to indemnification and defense and applicable law and court jurisdiction. An issue for state and local governments has been that social media sites like Facebook and Twitter have their own terms of service. Most employees are not aware that when they signed up, they agreed to those terms. As state and local governments have worked to develop their own usage terms, a key question is whose rules prevail? The federal government resolved its issues with Facebook, YouTube, Flickr, Vimeo and blip.tv through mutual agreements regarding liability, endorsements, freedom of information and governing laws. In 2011, through the efforts of the National Association of State Chief Information Officers (NASCIO) and a group of lawyers, deputy state CIOs, and technology and policy professionals, Facebook modified its terms of service for state and local governments. Additional review of these and other legal issues is provided in Chapter 5.

Ads

For many years, governments have shied away from the practice of web advertising, wary of the potential challenge for equal opportunity from an undesirable company.

The gauntlet always has been "Who goes first?" to deal with any possible legal action. However, driven by current budget constraints and opportunities through new media, governments are now reconsidering what may be feasible avenues for advertising. Within the parameters of legally defined program focus, specific service areas and specific program co-sponsorships, governments are examining options for very targeted approaches to generate advertising revenue. PTI recently conducted a member survey regarding web advertising and will be providing an update on what governments currently are doing regarding this topic.

Accessibility

Accessibility is important to governments. This value applies to web services and to new Web 2.0 technologies and social media now being implemented. People with disabilities have a strong interest in access to and use of web and social media, as these tools can be a transformational resource for connectivity, social interaction and continued learning.

Most social media sites today are fairly accessible, but they also pose varied problems for many users. The primary issues with social media for people with disabilities are:

- CAPTCHAs (Completely Automated Public Turing test to tell Computers and Humans Apart – the distorted text image that users often are required to type)
- Authentication
- Navigation
- Alternatives
- Rich Internet Applications (inaccessible scripting)
- User Generated Content (especially photo and video)
- Keyboard Limitations (e.g. links)

The good news is social media providers have been and continue to collaborate with end users and developers to improve accessibility. For example, Facebook began working jointly with the American Foundation for the Blind in 2008, has an Accessibility Team and now provides audio CAPTCHAs, enabling a screen reading user to register. Flickr has an Accessibility Lab. Open "Hack Days" with developers and disabled social media users have proven to be important sources of new ideas and technologies, and generated ongoing projects for social media providers.

There are useful, alternative user interfaces for some sites, especially for large sites such as Facebook and Twitter, and social media mobile applications are addressing disability issues. There also are a number of tools available now, such as:

- Accessible Twitter,[25] which is a web application that enables users with disabilities and limited technology to use Twitter, or simply "Tweet";
- Tweet Assist,[26] an Android application that is designed to make Twitter more accessible, with a simplified layout with large text and buttons for easier navigation and voice recognition.
- Easy YouTube,[27] a YouTube video downloader, with single click non-intrusive direct download buttons for FLV, 3GP, MP3, MP4, 720p HD and 1080p Full-HD qualities; and
- Easy YouTube Caption Creator,[28] designed to make it very simple to create a caption text file (.sub format) that can be added to YouTube video files that have been uploaded.

People with disabilities actively participate in numerous forums and social media sites to share tips, discuss problems and solutions, and work together towards more accessible social media tools.

There are several easy actions governments can take to improve accessibility on their social media sites:

- Provide captions for videos
- Title photographs
- Avoid abbreviations and text messaging shortcuts in status updates
- Ensure that the information posted is available through another channel that is accessible

One gap for disabled users is training in using social media tools, especially with the regular changes and updates that occur. A value-adding endeavor for government, especially local, is to provide training – at senior centers and other public facilities or through web-based video – to their residents on how to use social media or to update when social media providers make significant changes to their platforms. Governments can partner with their relevant agencies, boards or commissions to make the training available.

Portability and Interoperability

Multi-channel communications are a foundation of government efforts for engaging citizens through channel of choice and for achieving greater efficiencies by offloading customer calls to self-service and integrated systems. Along with the benefits of multi-channel options are the challenges of interoperability, data quality, portability and seamless delivery across systems.

Portability and interoperability can have different meanings and significance, depending on whether you are a government focused on efficiencies in Web 2.0 and social media endeavors, a social media provider or developer or the end user.

Interoperability refers to the ability to share data, from software and hardware on different machines and with different vendors through different networks. Portability refers to the capacity to utilize software or an application in multiple platforms. Interoperability is important enough that many groups, such as the W3C, collaborate with industry leaders worldwide to establish standards to ensure portability and interoperability for Web and mobile browsers and social media platforms. The main aim of standardization is to enable interoperability in a multi-vendor, multi-network, multi-service environment. A good Web 2.0 example of interoperability is RSS feeds, which, through the use of XML (Extensible Markup Language), can be interpreted on most platforms, including mobile phones.

Social media users are communicating their interest in being able to interchange their personal data, list of friends and other information on multiple applications. In order to utilize several Web 2.0 and social media platforms with the same application, portability is the key issue for development cost reduction. The downside of interoperability and portability within social networking involves identity, data authentication and protection of personal information, and discussions are underway regarding best practices, options such as OpenID and OAuth and data portability.

Great Example from the State of California

A good example of a government application with interoperability is the State of California's mobile website, m.ca.gov, as illustrated in Figure 21[29] (see next page). California's mobile website is comprised of more than 40 web-based mobile applications from across state government agencies. The site provides broad access to a variety of government services and information for most mobile phones with Internet access, many of which are interactive with Web 2.0 functionalities like Twitter and Facebook. A mobile user can either type in m.ca.gov in their browser or visit the California state portal (www.ca.gov) and be automatically redirected to the mobile site. Users can click to call or email agencies, get directions, or look up quick information, such as tax refund status. It is not necessary to download any of the application from an app store to use the mobile site. The site uses location-aware technology to pinpoint a user's specific location and provide the nearest government locations or other popular local and state resources (e.g., parks, hospitals, schools, current traffic conditions) in the immediate vicinity.

▶ All of the data that appears in the mobile apps is retrieved from a centralized knowledge base. Each agency is responsible for keeping its information updated, so the mobile site can retrieve it. Google Fusion Tables allows for instant viewing and the data is instantly enabled for use with application programming interface access to reuse the data (i.e., ready for mapping, mashups, and apps) in new and different ways.

▶ The mobile apps also use the phone's built-in GPS capabilities to detect a user's current location. The apps integrate with Google Maps, for example, locating offices on a map and giving turn-by-turn directions.

▶ All of the mobile apps can be viewed across multiple platforms and devices. The underlying technology is Google Fusion Tables, which allows data management and sharing and visualizing information in the cloud. It helps the state seamlessly merge data from disparate sources to the mobile site. There is no need to hook into agency databases, set up firewalls, or build expensive databases.

▶ Because of the underlying technology, applications are quick to produce – each taking as little as six hours to complete once an agency has decided which data to include in its app. In comparison, the CA.gov Locator (iPhone app) that was created in 2009, required two to three months development time, only runs on iPhones, required specialized mobile skills not available in-house, and required a lengthy approval process at the iTunes Store (see Figure 21, page 51) .

Open Data

Open data is becoming a key component of citizen demand and government efforts for transparency, accountability and efficiency. This means greater collaboration with citizens, businesses and other agencies to ensure that shared data is current, accurate and accessible. Mobile platforms, especially with better location precision, are facilitating this transformation. Open data empowers citizens to hold government accountable for the use of taxpayer money, provides access to important business development information, enables government to both provide and obtain specific and current information in emergencies, and assists in targeting relevant data for diverse citizen needs, interests

Figure 21. State of California

and geographic locations. Tracking the use of open data helps governments to identify priorities of the people and groups they serve, improving decision making and service delivery through better analytics. For maximum effectiveness, the evolving process for open data should focus government on what is most beneficial for social and economic development, rather than what is easiest to implement from a technological perspective.

Another Great Example from New York City

In their 2011 ROAD MAP,[30] the City of New York established several targeted goals in their plan for open government:

By unlocking important public information and supporting policies of Open Government, New York City will further expand access to services, enable innovation that improves the lives of New Yorkers, and increase transparency and efficiency.

1. Develop nyc Platform, an Open Government framework featuring APIs for City data

2. Launch a central hub for engaging and cultivating feedback from the developer community

3. Introduce visualization tools that make data more accessible to the public

4. Launch App Wishlists to support a needs-based ecosystem of innovation

5. Launch an official New York City Apps hub

Moving Forward

A critical driver for good policies, portability, interoperability and open data is that information and data need to be consistent across all channels of communication, as well as appropriate and accurate. As Web 2.0 and social media usage continues to explode, local and state governments progress when they utilize defined plans, policies and processes to address access, consistency, flexibility and manageability.

Going Beyond Output Measures

Governments have been measuring performance for many years, varying from huge federal documents to designated sections in local government annual budgets. There have been regular waves in emphasis, but core metrics traditionally focus on outputs, efficiency and effectiveness; that is, how many, what was the unit cost and what were citizen satisfaction levels. Over the years, government performance measures also tended to focus on operational services levels, such as three days to fix a pothole, or on program success, such as a 35 percent increase in graduation. The challenge always has been to balance the need for meaningful measures with the capacity to easily capture the data.

A new challenge exists with Web 2.0 and civic media tools, since many governments are quickly utilizing the new technologies and platforms and because most state and local governments have not gone beyond output measures – the number of followers or fans or friends or views.

Why You Should Measure

IMPROVED PERFORMANCE

- Identify & Respond to Citizen Expectations & Priorities
- Maximize Resources within Budget Limitations
- Go Where Citizens Go & Benefit from Collective Intelligence
- Determine the Value & Success of the Tool
- Meet Regulatory Demands
- Establish Accountability & Transparency

The reason for measuring performance is always to improve performance. Web 2.0 and civic media provide new channels for citizens to submit comments, discuss issues and share their expectations and priorities. Many platforms are free, extend outreach and streamline communications with minimal costs. Gathering performance and citizen data can help prove a case to support a project, program or yes vote. Using the tools most used by citizens increases access and input. In some cases, public, web-based performance reports are required by regulatory agencies, such as in transportation, energy, finance and grant funding. When governments both track performance and share results, accountability and transparency are increased, thus building trust in government for the use of resources. Data also trumps inaccurate assignment of blame and supposition for performance shortcomings.

Five Tips for Types of Metrics

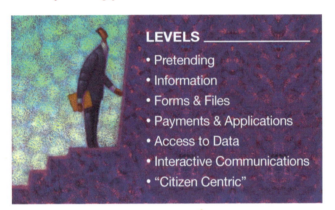

LEVELS _____
- Pretending
- Information
- Forms & Files
- Payments & Applications
- Access to Data
- Interactive Communications
- "Citizen Centric"

To move beyond the "pretending" level and make real progress towards the "citizen centric" level in the use of Web 2.0 and civic media, set performance metrics that:

1. Relate back to **communication goals**.
2. Go beyond output measures – page views/followers – to **real program metrics**, such as offline actions – percentage increases in event attendance and program registrations; drives to specific web pages; reduction in specific type calls to your 311.
3. Consider four areas to measure: **exposure, engagement, influence and action**.
4. In addition to standard return on investment and metrics such as cost per unique visitor, focus on **impact** and **value measures** (e.g. comment-to-post ratios, percent of new followers/likers).

CHAPTER 4 : GOING BEYOND OUTPUT MEASURES

5. Balance with tracking options within the social media tool itself, CRMs and free and commercial analytics services.

Remember, governments are not focused on sales – but on increasing **citizen engagement, government accountability, and responsive and cost-efficient communication channels and services.**[31]

For the four areas to measure, performance to track includes:

1. **Exposure:** impressions and views; discussions; increase/decrease in followers and likers
2. **Engagement:** interaction rate, posted comments and questions; reduction in call center calls on topic; number of re-tweets; bookmarks, votes, likes; increase/decrease in number of subscribers; increase/decrease in participation rates
3. **Influence:** documented change in opinions and attitudes; ratings and reviews
4. **Action:** attendance at promoted events or program registrations; visits to linked websites; votes for or against; accomplished program goals

Criteria for Good Analytics

▶ Directly tied to goals/objectives

▶ Are strategy/initiative-based or process-based (organization or individual ownership follows)

▶ Are relevant to work activities

▶ Are clearly defined with targets (units, how measured, baseline/history)

▶ Can be updated on a regular frequency and data collection is available or possible

Pitfalls for Good Performance Measures

▶ Too many to manage

▶ No relevance to business processes

▶ Little impact on work activities

▶ Too complex to understand

▶ Impossible to collect data or more trouble than it's worth

▶ Easiest to track and measure

▶ Poorly defined and inconsistent in how measured

- Viewed as "out of my control" for making adjustments or improvements
- Not linked to goals and objectives

A Process Example

Government public safety agencies actively use Web 2.0 and civic media applications in communicating with citizens, collecting and sharing data with citizens and partner agencies, and in all aspects of disaster recovery. Many state and local governments use Facebook, Twitter, mashups and mapping, alerts and mobile applications for emergency communications and broad emergency management participation.

While testifying before a Senate Homeland Security panel in May 2011, FEMA Administrator Craig Fugate noted that social media was essential to disaster communication efforts "because it helps to facilitate the vital two-way communication between emergency management agencies and the public, and it allows us to quickly and specifically share information with state and local governments as well as the public."

Social media has a prevalent role in FEMA's disaster response, but Fugate also emphasized the importance of social media being used as a true communication tool as opposed to one used primarily for making static announcements. "I often say that individuals, families and communities are our nation's 'first' first responders," Fugate testified. "Through the use of social media, we can disseminate important information to individuals and communities, while also receiving essential real-time updates from those with first-hand awareness."[32]

Emergency management provides a good example of identifying action-related communication goals to measure:

Situation Awareness[33]

- Were citizens better informed and prepared and did they improve their prevention efforts?
- Were we better able to collect, share and distribute timely, multi-media and helpful information on what happened and who was impacted?
- Were we better able to collect, share and distribute timely and helpful information on the specific locations with damage?
- Were we able to coordinate information to know when services would be restored?

Expert Knowledge & Advice

- ❱ Did civic media tools help identify risks?
- ❱ Were we better able to develop mitigation strategies?
- ❱ Were we better able to coordinate and distribute health warnings?
- ❱ Did we successfully target, communicate with and assist vulnerable populations?

News and Emerging Information

- ❱ Were we better able to collect, share and provide timely information for local news reports?
- ❱ Were we better able to collect, share and provide timely photos of damage?
- ❱ Were we better able to collect, share and provide traffic impact information?
- ❱ Did we receive eyewitness accounts?
- ❱ Were we actively involved in incident articles and analysis?

Recovery Assistance

- ❱ Were we better able to collect, share and provide timely shelter locations?
- ❱ Did we provide timely government assistance?
- ❱ Were we better able to enlist community support?
- ❱ Were we better able to mobilize and coordinate volunteer networks?
- ❱ Were we better able to identify and communication help needed?

A government public safety agency could select one or two priority areas from each of these emergency management focus areas; establish qualitative and quantifiable performance goals, select metrics that will answer the questions above, set targets; and then track actual performance to clearly determine if Web 2.0 and civic media applications are helping to accomplish the desired results. This process can be applied to other service areas to facilitate identifying meaningful focus areas, goals and performance metrics.

Analytics Tools

In addition to the desired program and service metrics, it is beneficial to track and analyze visitor traffic and use of Web 2.0 or civic media applications to better understand the communication preferences and patterns of a particular community and to build on those that maximize outreach and engagement. Often, instant feedback is obtained on interactive tools through user-posted comments, questions and complaints. Some platforms have built-in traffic analytics, like Facebook, which provides insights with data and graphs for posts, users and interactions, and YouTube, which delivers data such as views, popularity and demographics.

There currently are a range of analytics tools, many of which are free, open source and easy-to-use online dashboards in which you enter your social media name/URL and data is instantly generated. Because the private sector is very interested in sales, marketing and consumer behavior, a variety of options are available, depending on the depth of information you want. Google Analytics is very popular, along with a number of plug-ins it provides for other social media, like WordPress for blogs. Google Analytics enables measurement of site engagement goals and cross-channel and multi-media tracking, including mobile websites, apps and web-enabled mobile devices. Another tool, Hootsuite, provides a dashboard for multiple social media networks and can generate custom reports from over 30 individual report modules. TweetStats is a very quick process to obtain activity data for Twitter sites. Some other measurement tools are Yahoo Web Analytics, Stat Counter, Free Stats and Site Meter. These are just a few of the multitude of traffic and usage measurement services for Web 2.0 and social media.

The following is an example of two of Facebook insights, one with data on users and interactions and another showing impressions, or views of wall postings.

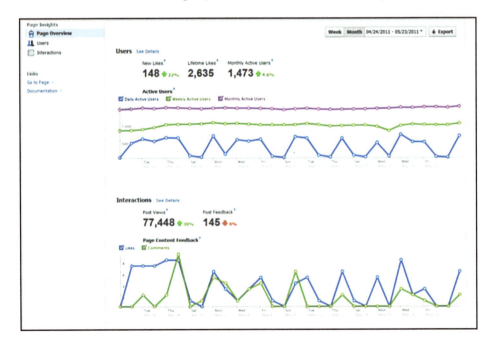

Page Posts[7]

Message	Posted ▼	Impressions	Feedback
City Invites Community to Events and Programs in...	May 20 at 11:36am	1,506	0.20 %
Beach to Bay Event will Require Temporary Street and Lane...	May 20 at 11:07am	1,558	0 %
City Holiday Schedules For Memorial Day 2011	May 19 at 3:26pm	1,781	0.056 %
Glass Recycling Event to be Held Saturday, May 21, 2011	May 18 at 4:23pm	2,127	0.094 %
Corpus Christi Police Explorers Hold Open House	May 18 at 3:52pm	2,119	0.094 %
Water Department to Kick Off "Don't Waste the Wet Stuff"...	May 18 at 1:16pm	2,033	0.15 %
City Council District 3 Runoff Election to be Held...	May 18 at 9:59am	1,903	0 %
Laguna Shores Road Now Reopen	May 18 at 9:58am	1,805	0.39 %
Corpus Christi Firefighters to be Recognized for Life...	May 16 at 9:24am	2,018	0.15 %
Corpus Christi-Nueces County Public Health District Offers...	May 13 at 3:59pm	2,125	0.094 %

Current Government Performance Measurement Practices

In a 2010 survey of local governments conducted by PTI, *Web 2.0 Metrics and Business Intelligence in Local Government,* the majority of respondents indicated they do not have established metrics for their Web 2.0 and civic/social media applications. The following are some of the survey results:

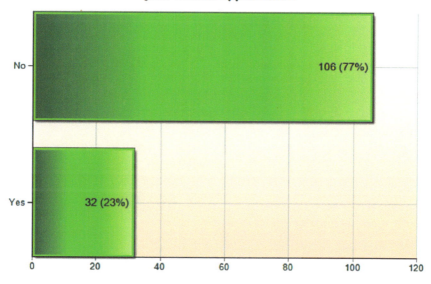

Do you currently have a system to capture usage and traffic metrics from your Web 2.0 applications?

No — 106 (77%)

Yes — 32 (23%)

0   20   40   60   80   100   120

If you currently do not have a system to capture usage and traffic metrics from your Web 2.0 applications, do you plan to implement a system within the next twelve months?

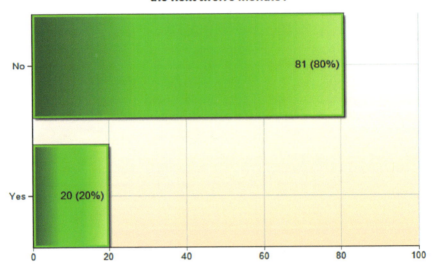

If you do not have or plan to use Web 2.0 metrics please select the reasons why (select all that apply):

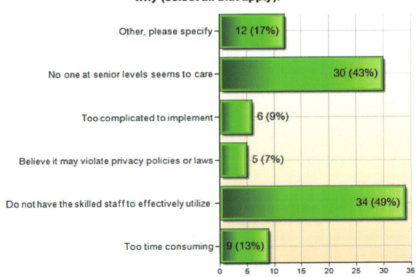

CHAPTER 4 : GOING BEYOND OUTPUT MEASURES

As illustrated in the above charts, most governments are not tracking performance of their Web 2.0 and civic media applications, with the primary reasons being the lack of "skilled staff to effectively utilize" and senior staff level interest.

In PTI's 2011 Web 2.0 State and Local Government Awards and Recognition program, 37 percent of the award applicants, representing diverse communities, did not have established performance metrics for their Web 2.0 and civic media applications. Thirty-one percent had established traffic and usage metrics; 17 percent had traffic and response time metrics and five percent had established traffic and results metrics.

Several had quantifiable efficiency measures, such as calculated ROI for the application, cost savings through improvement suggestions generated and implemented (one county had savings of almost $1.2 million through implementation of 85 ideas); unit cost reductions through offloading calls to self-service applications; cost savings through new system integration, interoperability and portability; and reduction in staffing and time requirements. A number of performance metrics were online and mobile extensions of their 311/contact centers response time targets (contact, resolution, close and cycle times) and meeting service level agreements. One city had results-oriented Facebook metrics for funds raised, volunteers enlisted and a re-built park.

In addition to views, traffic measures included subscriber counts, new likes, increase in monthly active users, availability, bounce rate and pushed tweets.

Another value related to government performance management and the use of Web 2.0 and civic media tools is the opportunity to gain informal performance assessments from citizens about perceptions of the organization or about specific departments/ agencies and services provided through user postings, questions, comments and complaints. Civic media can connect government to the "collective crowd."

Some Great Resources

The federal government provides excellent resources for social media at its HowTo.Gov website,[34] with information on the best uses of social media and tips on web analytics for measuring usability and participation, as well as how to evaluate mission achievement. It recommends effectiveness metrics, using both quantitative and qualitative data and separated into several broad categories:

"Customer Focus and Experience" metrics, which focus on the user:

- ◗ Audience analysis
- ◗ Measuring customer satisfaction
- ◗ Conducting usability testing (goes to "Usability & Design" section)
- ◗ Analyzing web logs
- ◗ Reviewing links regularly

"Quality and Compliance" metrics:

- ◗ Measuring technical performance
- ◗ Ensuring accessibility / Section 508

"Recognition" metrics:

- ◗ Applying for awards

"The Voice of the People"

In her book, *Listening to the Public, Adding the Voices of the People to Government Performance Measurement and Reporting,* Berman, reveals that, after much research into citizen evaluation of local government performance, the most "consistent and compelling finding was that people judge government performance in ways that differ markedly from the standard measures that governments use to evaluate themselves."[35] Citizens focus more on quality and effectiveness of government's activities than on the inputs and outputs typically emphasized by government. Berman reports that people discuss and see government services differently from the way government is arranged and responds. They view government – and services – across departments and agencies. A significant element of Web 2.0 and civic media is that applications often are more service oriented than many websites that are segmented by departments/agencies. Web 2.0 and social media tools frequently provide cross-agency information, data access and opportunities for citizen feedback from their perspectives.

The Power of Web 2.0

Moving Forward

The power of Web 2.0 and social media has been demonstrated in a variety of ways – whether it is real-time sharing of photos, mapping and on-the-scene updates during a threatening fire, a bridge collapse, or a campus shooting; or just some amazing videos gone viral; or a local community raising funds and volunteers to rebuild a park. Access to and usage of these technologies and tools will continue their compounding expansion. Governments will join in, with a choice of approaching it as a check-off, a "cool tool," or a valid tool to engage active citizen participation, demonstrate transparency to rebuild trust, and achieve improved efficiencies. To be successful with the latter approach, governments must make upfront decisions to establish metrics and track actual performance and then utilize the data to change course, improve or celebrate.

CHAPTER 5

Legal & Ethical Considerations

There is a fast-growing list of state and local governments who are signing up for social media applications where citizens can assess on desktop computers, laptops, smartphones, PDAs, and even tablet computers. After all, it makes sense when one considers the enormous adoption rate of the general public. No one purchases a computer or mobile device to connect with government – but if a large segment of the public already has and uses such technology, it makes perfect sense to capitalize on this growing trend. Nearly all of the web-based services are "free" to the public as are most mobile apps – but even "free" comes with a price. There is always a cost to staff, train, manage and maintain.

One area that often escapes scrutiny is legal and ethical considerations. In our eagerness and impatience, people all too often click the bottom button to accept new downloads as well as new online products and services. We rarely read the long scroll bar that explains "rights and responsibilities" as we quickly jump to the bottom and click to "agree". Making matters worse, people are often agreeing, not only the terms and conditions, but also agreeing and attesting to the fact we actually read all the legalese – when in fact we did not. For the overwhelming majority, this rarely, if ever, leads to a serious problem. In addition, for most of us, reading a terms of service clause is like reading an elevator safety certificate. For state and local governments this may be a more serious matter.

As more state and local governments turn to various social media platforms such as Facebook, Twitter, and YouTube, many public managers have blindly signed online agreements without much thought to possible legal consequences. Many have stated that they simply had no choice, there were no other options, and there was no way one government entity would ever get a giant like Facebook to make any changes to its standard terms of service agreements. This purpose of this chapter is to help heighten awareness of two related issues, legal and ethical considerations.

If you were to print out Google's Terms of Services, (owner of YouTube) you would be printing out no less than 15 pages. Facebook has no less than five pages and Twitter has no less than seven. Adding to the complexity, each of the three social media companies named have numerous links in each of their terms of service pages that can take you to dozens of other forms and polices.

As individuals, we sign such terms and are agreeing to them whether we really agree or not or if we read them or not. When governments sign up for a social media application such as Twitter or Facebook the question that comes up is to what extent the laws of government may or may not be subjugated. Issues that often arise are those involving *privacy, user safety, account security, people's rights, content ownership*, and lastly, *disputes*.

When one posts an official government – produced video on YouTube, who owns the copyright? What happens if there is a breach of security? Moreover, should there be a dispute between a government entity and a social media site – what is the mechanism for a resolution? The answers may surprise you. Anything posted on YouTube can be shared by anyone – regardless of copyright, and lastly, dispute resolutions are to be resolved in the state in which the social media site is headquartered, not where the complaint originated. Most of the popular social media companies are located in California, thus making taking legal action a rather expensive process with just travel costs alone. However, many are also located in other countries.

When it comes to "content" companies like Google state that the user retains the copyright. However, in another section it states "By submitting, posting or displaying the content you give Google a perpetual, irrevocable, worldwide, royalty-free, and non-exclusive license to reproduce, adapt, modify, translate, publish, publicly perform, publicly display and distribute any Content which you submit, post or display on or through, the Services. This license is for the sole purpose of enabling Google to display, distribute and promote the Services and may be revoked for certain Services as defined in the Additional Terms of those Services".

Critics of Facebook argue that once something is posted on Facebook, it gets full control of the content, raising the question: Who owns content and under what conditions does this change?

In 2009, the Federal government was able to negotiate an amended terms of service agreement for agencies with Facebook. It did not take long for the other leading social media sites to follow in the path of Facebook. A coalition of federal agencies led by GSA's Office of Citizen Services have been actively working on developing model Terms of Serve Agreements so that any Federal agency would not have to start from scratch.

The National Association of State Chief Information Officers (NASCIO) formed an ad hoc group of lawyers, deputy state CIOs, and technology and policy professionals to develop similar agreements for state and local governments. In January 2011, NASCIO announced that, "After lengthy discussions involving members of the National Association of State Chief Information Officers (NASCIO) Social Media Legal workgroup and the National Association of Attorneys General (NAAG), Facebook has revised the standard terms of service to be provided to state and local governments through its 'Pages' agreement. The revised terms resolve a series of legal issues identified by states in Facebook's standard terms of service and are available for immediate use."

Doug Robinson, NASCIO's executive director, indicated that this agreement will remove significant barriers and enable broader adoption and leveraging of social media tools that enhance communications with constituents. He expects that the Facebook agreement will be used as a model, as the NASCIO workgroup continues their efforts to produce similar agreements with other social media providers.

"Facebook has specifically agreed to modify the provisions of its terms and conditions to:

- Strike the indemnity clause except to the extent indemnity is allowed by a state's constitution or law;

- Strike language requiring that legal disputes be venued in California courts and adjudicated under California law;

- Require that a public agency include language directing consumers to its official Web site prominently on any Facebook page; and,

- Encourage amicable resolution between public entities and Facebook over any disputes."

The modifications immediately applied to state and local government agencies already on Facebook. [36]

State and local governments have come to rely on social/civic media services as a means to broadcast information regarding special events, emergencies, and other civic matters. However, when a public official wishes to state an opinion or simply weigh in on an issue, is this something that would violate a Sunshine Law provision? One must ask if comments on official matters considered part of the public record? Each government jurisdiction operates under its own laws, regulations, and sometimes, State law. Most were written well before 2004, prior to the creation and adoption of social media, as we know it today.

Problems with social/civic media are often found when people use the same medium to "broadcast" back. After all, the main selling point of social media is citizen engagement, which by its nature is interactive. Yet, what happens when someone "friends" a politician or other public official and then turns around and uses all the contacts ("friends") to sell personal services like real estate or accounting services, or uses the contacts to endorse another candidate or weigh in on a particular issue? Some violations may manifest themselves as lapses in ethical judgment while others may be unlawful. What happens when someone posts inappropriate language or slanderous comments? This leads to the larger question, what internal policies are in place. Do such policies address issues such as employee usage, content management, content publishing, trouble-shooting/support, privacy, records management, security, authenticity, terms of use, rights of others, conflict of interest, content deletion, safety, monitoring to name a few? The appropriate government attorney must review social/civic media policies periodically. Citizens have enough to worry about; however, when social media sites are adopted for state and local government use the stakes are much higher. Of particular importance to many is how do social network sites and mobile applications protect one's identity and right to privacy? This is an area where sadly there are more questions than answers.

Moving Forward

Local government technology leaders are usually the best equipped to host or manage a civic media platform – but a high-level public information staff person should be responsible for message and content management. The third leg of the stool should be the municipal attorney, who needs to make certain that the state or local government is adequately protected under the law as well as the citizens who place their trust into the civic media system. So be careful where you click and what you click!

References

GSA Social Media Handbook
http://www.gsa.gov/graphics/staffoffices/socialmediahandbook.pdf

GSA Social Media Policy
http://www.gsa.gov/graphics/staffoffices/socialmediapolicy.pdf

How-To.Gov, Terms of Service Agreements with New Media Providers
http://www.usa.gov/webcontent/resources/tools/TOSagreemenst.shtml

IBM Social Media Guidelines
http://www.ibm.com/blogs/zz/en/guidelines.html

Intel Social Media Guidelines
http://www.intel.com/sites/sitewide/en_US/socialmedia.htm

International Chiefs of Police, Social Media Policy
http://www.tosback.org/timeline.php

Social Media and Web 2.0 in Government
http://www.usa.gov/webcontent/technology/other_tech.shtml

TOSS Back Terms of Service Tracker
http://www.tosback.org/timeline.php

Web 2 0 Governance Policies and Best Practices,
 http://socmed.pbworks.com/Web-2-0-Governance-Policies-and-Best-Practices

Web Content Mangers Forum, Terms of service Agreements
http://forum.webcontent.gov/Default.asp?page=TOS_agreements

Samples of Terms of Service Statements Found Online

Of course, terms of service and other conditions are always subject to change, and what is offered here is simply a sample. There is however, a great online service called Terms of Service Tracker that alerts a user whenever a social media company makes a change to their terms of service agreements. See http://www.tosback.org/timeline.php.

Google Terms of Service

Welcome to Google!
1. Your relationship with Google
   1.1 Your use of Google's products, software, services and web sites (referred to collectively as the "Services" in this document and excluding any services provided to you by Google under a separate written agreement) is subject to the terms of a legal agreement between you and Google. "Google" means Google Inc., whose principal place of business is at 1600 Amphitheatre Parkway, Mountain View, CA 94043, United States. This document explains how the agreement is made up, and sets out some of the terms of that agreement.
   1.2 Unless otherwise agreed in writing with Google, your agreement with Google will always include, at a minimum, the terms and conditions set out in this document. These are referred to below as the "Universal Terms".
   1.3 Your agreement with Google will also include the terms of any Legal Notices applicable to the Services, in addition to the Universal Terms. All of these are referred to below as the "Additional Terms". Where Additional Terms apply to a Service, these will be accessible for you to read either within, or through your use of, that Service.
   1.4 The Universal Terms, together with the Additional Terms, form a legally binding agreement between you and Google in relation to your use of the Services. It is important that you take the time to read them carefully. Collectively, this legal agreement is referred to below as the "Terms".
   1.5 If there is any contradiction between what the Additional Terms say and what the Universal Terms say, then the Additional Terms shall take precedence in relation to that Service.
2. Accepting the Terms
   2.1 In order to use the Services, you must first agree to the Terms. You may not use the Services if you do not accept the Terms.
   2.2 You can accept the Terms by:
     (A) clicking to accept or agree to the Terms, where this option is made available to you by Google in the user interface for any Service; or
     (B) by actually using the Services. In this case, you understand and agree that Google will treat your use of the Services as acceptance of the Terms from that point onwards.
   2.3 You may not use the Services and may not accept the Terms if (a) you are not of legal age to form a binding contract with Google, or (b) you are a person barred from receiving the Services under the laws of the United States or other countries including the country in which you are resident or from which you use the Services.
   2.4 Before you continue, you should print off or save a local copy of the Universal Terms for your records.

3. Language of the Terms
    3.1 Where Google has provided you with a translation of the English language version of the Terms, then you agree that the translation is provided for your convenience only and that the English language versions of the Terms will govern your relationship with Google.
    3.2 If there is any contradiction between what the English language version of the Terms says and what a translation says, then the English language version shall take precedence.
4. Provision of the Services by Google
    4.1 Google has subsidiaries and affiliated legal entities around the world ("Subsidiaries and Affiliates"). Sometimes, these companies will be providing the Services to you on behalf of Google itself. You acknowledge and agree that Subsidiaries and Affiliates will be entitled to provide the Services to you.
    4.2 Google is constantly innovating in order to provide the best possible experience for its users. You acknowledge and agree that the form and nature of the Services which Google provides may change from time to time without prior notice to you.
    4.3 As part of this continuing innovation, you acknowledge and agree that Google may stop (permanently or temporarily) providing the Services (or any features within the Services) to you or to users generally at Google's sole discretion, without prior notice to you. You may stop using the Services at any time. You do not need to specifically inform Google when you stop using the Services.
    4.4 You acknowledge and agree that if Google disables access to your account, you may be prevented from accessing the Services, your account details or any files or other content which is contained in your account.
    4.5 You acknowledge and agree that while Google may not currently have set a fixed upper limit on the number of transmissions you may send or receive through the Services or on the amount of storage space used for the provision of any Service, such fixed upper limits may be set by Google at any time, at Google's discretion.
5. Use of the Services by you
    5.1 In order to access certain Services, you may be required to provide information about yourself (such as identification or contact details) as part of the registration process for the Service, or as part of your continued use of the Services. You agree that any registration information you give to Google will always be accurate, correct and up to date.
    5.2 You agree to use the Services only for purposes that are permitted by (a) the Terms and (b) any applicable law, regulation or generally accepted practices or guidelines in the relevant jurisdictions (including any laws regarding the export of data or software to and from the United States or other relevant countries).
    5.3 You agree not to access (or attempt to access) any of the Services by any means other than through the interface that is provided by Google, unless you have been specifically allowed to do so in a separate agreement with Google. You specifically agree not to access (or attempt to access) any of the Services through any automated means (including use of scripts or web crawlers) and shall ensure that you comply with the instructions set out in any robots.txt file present on the Services.
    5.4 You agree that you will not engage in any activity that interferes with or disrupts the Services (or the servers and networks which are connected to the Services).
    5.5 Unless you have been specifically permitted to do so in a separate agreement with Google, you agree that you will not reproduce, duplicate, copy, sell, trade or resell the Services for any purpose.
    5.6 You agree that you are solely responsible for (and that Google has no responsibility to you or to any third party for) any breach of your obligations under the Terms and for the consequences (including any loss or damage which Google may suffer) of any such breach.
6. Your passwords and account security

6.1 You agree and understand that you are responsible for maintaining the confidentiality of passwords associated with any account you use to access the Services.

6.2 Accordingly, you agree that you will be solely responsible to Google for all activities that occur under your account.

6.3 If you become aware of any unauthorized use of your password or of your account, you agree to notify Google immediately at http://www.google.com/support/accounts/bin/answer.py?answer=58585.

7. Privacy and your personal information

7.1 For information about Google's data protection practices, please read Google's privacy policy at http://www.google.com/privacy.html. This policy explains how Google treats your personal information, and protects your privacy, when you use the Services.

7.2 You agree to the use of your data in accordance with Google's privacy policies.

8. Content in the Services

8.1 You understand that all information (such as data files, written text, computer software, music, audio files or other sounds, photographs, videos or other images) which you may have access to as part of, or through your use of, the Services are the sole responsibility of the person from which such content originated. All such information is referred to below as the "Content".

8.2 You should be aware that Content presented to you as part of the Services, including but not limited to advertisements in the Services and sponsored Content within the Services may be protected by intellectual property rights which are owned by the sponsors or advertisers who provide that Content to Google (or by other persons or companies on their behalf). You may not modify, rent, lease, loan, sell, distribute or create derivative works based on this Content (either in whole or in part) unless you have been specifically told that you may do so by Google or by the owners of that Content, in a separate agreement.

8.3 Google reserves the right (but shall have no obligation) to pre-screen, review, flag, filter, modify, refuse or remove any or all Content from any Service. For some of the Services, Google may provide tools to filter out explicit sexual content. These tools include the SafeSearch preference settings (see http://www.google.com/help/customize.html#safe). In addition, there are commercially available services and software to limit access to material that you may find objectionable.

8.4 You understand that by using the Services you may be exposed to Content that you may find offensive, indecent or objectionable and that, in this respect, you use the Services at your own risk.

8.5 You agree that you are solely responsible for (and that Google has no responsibility to you or to any third party for) any Content that you create, transmit or display while using the Services and for the consequences of your actions (including any loss or damage which Google may suffer) by doing so.

9. Proprietary rights

9.1 You acknowledge and agree that Google (or Google's licensors) own all legal right, title and interest in and to the Services, including any intellectual property rights which subsist in the Services (whether those rights happen to be registered or not, and wherever in the world those rights may exist). You further acknowledge that the Services may contain information which is designated confidential by Google and that you shall not disclose such information without Google's prior written consent.

9.2 Unless you have agreed otherwise in writing with Google, nothing in the Terms gives you a right to use any of Google's trade names, trade marks, service marks, logos, domain names, and other distinctive brand features.

9.3 If you have been given an explicit right to use any of these brand features in a separate written agreement with Google, then you agree that your use of such features shall be in compliance with that agreement, any applicable provisions of the Terms, and Google's brand feature use guidelines as updated from time to time. These guidelines can be viewed online at http://www.google.com/

permissions/guidelines.html (or such other URL as Google may provide for this purpose from time to time).

9.4 Other than the limited license set forth in Section 11, Google acknowledges and agrees that it obtains no right, title or interest from you (or your licensors) under these Terms in or to any Content that you submit, post, transmit or display on, or through, the Services, including any intellectual property rights which subsist in that Content (whether those rights happen to be registered or not, and wherever in the world those rights may exist). Unless you have agreed otherwise in writing with Google, you agree that you are responsible for protecting and enforcing those rights and that Google has no obligation to do so on your behalf.

9.5 You agree that you shall not remove, obscure, or alter any proprietary rights notices (including copyright and trade mark notices) which may be affixed to or contained within the Services.

9.6 Unless you have been expressly authorized to do so in writing by Google, you agree that in using the Services, you will not use any trade mark, service mark, trade name, logo of any company or organization in a way that is likely or intended to cause confusion about the owner or authorized user of such marks, names or logos.

10. License from Google

10.1 Google gives you a personal, worldwide, royalty-free, non-assignable and non-exclusive license to use the software provided to you by Google as part of the Services as provided to you by Google (referred to as the "Software" below). This license is for the sole purpose of enabling you to use and enjoy the benefit of the Services as provided by Google, in the manner permitted by the Terms.

10.2 You may not (and you may not permit anyone else to) copy, modify, create a derivative work of, reverse engineer, decompile or otherwise attempt to extract the source code of the Software or any part thereof, unless this is expressly permitted or required by law, or unless you have been specifically told that you may do so by Google, in writing.

10.3 Unless Google has given you specific written permission to do so, you may not assign (or grant a sub-license of) your rights to use the Software, grant a security interest in or over your rights to use the Software, or otherwise transfer any part of your rights to use the Software.

11. Content license from you

11.1 You retain copyright and any other rights you already hold in Content which you submit, post or display on or through, the Services. By submitting, posting or displaying the content you give Google a perpetual, irrevocable, worldwide, royalty-free, and non-exclusive license to reproduce, adapt, modify, translate, publish, publicly perform, publicly display and distribute any Content which you submit, post or display on or through, the Services. This license is for the sole purpose of enabling Google to display, distribute and promote the Services and may be revoked for certain Services as defined in the Additional Terms of those Services.

11.2 You agree that this license includes a right for Google to make such Content available to other companies, organizations or individuals with whom Google has relationships for the provision of syndicated services, and to use such Content in connection with the provision of those services.

11.3 You understand that Google, in performing the required technical steps to provide the Services to our users, may (a) transmit or distribute your Content over various public networks and in various media; and (b) make such changes to your Content as are necessary to conform and adapt that Content to the technical requirements of connecting networks, devices, services or media. You agree that this license shall permit Google to take these actions.

11.4 You confirm and warrant to Google that you have all the rights, power and authority necessary to grant the above license.

12. Software updates

12.1 The Software which you use may automatically download and install updates from time to time from Google. These updates are designed to improve, enhance and further develop the Services and may take the form of bug fixes, enhanced functions, new software modules and completely new versions. You agree to receive such updates (and permit Google to deliver these to you) as part of your use of the Services.

13. Ending your relationship with Google

13.1 The Terms will continue to apply until terminated by either you or Google as set out below.

13.2 If you want to terminate your legal agreement with Google, you may do so by (a) notifying Google at any time and (b) closing your accounts for all of the Services which you use, where Google has made this option available to you. Your notice should be sent, in writing, to Google's address which is set out at the beginning of these Terms.

13.3 Google may at any time, terminate its legal agreement with you if:

(A) you have breached any provision of the Terms (or have acted in manner which clearly shows that you do not intend to, or are unable to comply with the provisions of the Terms); or

(B) Google is required to do so by law (for example, where the provision of the Services to you is, or becomes, unlawful); or

(C) the partner with whom Google offered the Services to you has terminated its relationship with Google or ceased to offer the Services to you; or

(D) Google is transitioning to no longer providing the Services to users in the country in which you are resident or from which you use the service; or

(E) the provision of the Services to you by Google is, in Google's opinion, no longer commercially viable.

13.4 Nothing in this Section shall affect Google's rights regarding provision of Services under Section 4 of the Terms.

13.5 When these Terms come to an end, all of the legal rights, obligations and liabilities that you and Google have benefited from, been subject to (or which have accrued over time whilst the Terms have been in force) or which are expressed to continue indefinitely, shall be unaffected by this cessation, and the provisions of paragraph 20.7 shall continue to apply to such rights, obligations and liabilities indefinitely.

14. EXCLUSION OF WARRANTIES

14.1 NOTHING IN THESE TERMS, INCLUDING SECTIONS 14 AND 15, SHALL EXCLUDE OR LIMIT GOOGLE'S WARRANTY OR LIABILITY FOR LOSSES WHICH MAY NOT BE LAWFULLY EXCLUDED OR LIMITED BY APPLICABLE LAW. SOME JURISDICTIONS DO NOT ALLOW THE EXCLUSION OF CERTAIN WARRANTIES OR CONDITIONS OR THE LIMITATION OR EXCLU-SION OF LIABILITY FOR LOSS OR DAMAGE CAUSED BY NEGLIGENCE, BREACH OF CON-TRACT OR BREACH OF IMPLIED TERMS, OR INCIDENTAL OR CONSEQUENTIAL DAMAGES. ACCORDINGLY, ONLY THE LIMITATIONS WHICH ARE LAWFUL IN YOUR JURISDICTION WILL APPLY TO YOU AND OUR LIABILITY WILL BE LIMITED TO THE MAXIMUM EXTENT PERMITTED BY LAW.

14.2 YOU EXPRESSLY UNDERSTAND AND AGREE THAT YOUR USE OF THE SERVICES IS AT YOUR SOLE RISK AND THAT THE SERVICES ARE PROVIDED "AS IS" AND "AS AVAILABLE."

14.3 IN PARTICULAR, GOOGLE, ITS SUBSIDIARIES AND AFFILIATES, AND ITS LICENSORS DO NOT REPRESENT OR WARRANT TO YOU THAT:

(A) YOUR USE OF THE SERVICES WILL MEET YOUR REQUIREMENTS,

(B) YOUR USE OF THE SERVICES WILL BE UNINTERRUPTED, TIMELY, SECURE OR FREE FROM ERROR,

(C) ANY INFORMATION OBTAINED BY YOU AS A RESULT OF YOUR USE OF THE SERVICES WILL BE ACCURATE OR RELIABLE, AND

(D) THAT DEFECTS IN THE OPERATION OR FUNCTIONALITY OF ANY SOFTWARE PROVIDED TO YOU AS PART OF THE SERVICES WILL BE CORRECTED.

14.4 ANY MATERIAL DOWNLOADED OR OTHERWISE OBTAINED THROUGH THE USE OF THE SERVICES IS DONE AT YOUR OWN DISCRETION AND RISK AND THAT YOU WILL BE SOLELY RESPONSIBLE FOR ANY DAMAGE TO YOUR COMPUTER SYSTEM OR OTHER DEVICE OR LOSS OF DATA THAT RESULTS FROM THE DOWNLOAD OF ANY SUCH MATERIAL.

14.5 NO ADVICE OR INFORMATION, WHETHER ORAL OR WRITTEN, OBTAINED BY YOU FROM GOOGLE OR THROUGH OR FROM THE SERVICES SHALL CREATE ANY WARRANTY NOT EXPRESSLY STATED IN THE TERMS.

14.6 GOOGLE FURTHER EXPRESSLY DISCLAIMS ALL WARRANTIES AND CONDITIONS OF ANY KIND, WHETHER EXPRESS OR IMPLIED, INCLUDING, BUT NOT LIMITED TO THE IMPLIED WARRANTIES AND CONDITIONS OF MERCHANTABILITY, FITNESS FOR A PARTICULAR PURPOSE AND NON-INFRINGEMENT.

15. LIMITATION OF LIABILITY

15.1 SUBJECT TO OVERALL PROVISION IN PARAGRAPH 14.1 ABOVE, YOU EXPRESSLY UNDERSTAND AND AGREE THAT GOOGLE, ITS SUBSIDIARIES AND AFFILIATES, AND ITS LICENSORS SHALL NOT BE LIABLE TO YOU FOR:

(A) ANY DIRECT, INDIRECT, INCIDENTAL, SPECIAL CONSEQUENTIAL OR EXEMPLARY DAMAGES WHICH MAY BE INCURRED BY YOU, HOWEVER CAUSED AND UNDER ANY THEORY OF LIABILITY.. THIS SHALL INCLUDE, BUT NOT BE LIMITED TO, ANY LOSS OF PROFIT (WHETHER INCURRED DIRECTLY OR INDIRECTLY), ANY LOSS OF GOODWILL OR BUSINESS REPUTATION, ANY LOSS OF DATA SUFFERED, COST OF PROCUREMENT OF SUBSTITUTE GOODS OR SERVICES, OR OTHER INTANGIBLE LOSS;

(B) ANY LOSS OR DAMAGE WHICH MAY BE INCURRED BY YOU, INCLUDING BUT NOT LIMITED TO LOSS OR DAMAGE AS A RESULT OF:

(I) ANY RELIANCE PLACED BY YOU ON THE COMPLETENESS, ACCURACY OR EXISTENCE OF ANY ADVERTISING, OR AS A RESULT OF ANY RELATIONSHIP OR TRANSACTION BETWEEN YOU AND ANY ADVERTISER OR SPONSOR WHOSE ADVERTISING APPEARS ON THE SERVICES;

(II) ANY CHANGES WHICH GOOGLE MAY MAKE TO THE SERVICES, OR FOR ANY PERMANENT OR TEMPORARY CESSATION IN THE PROVISION OF THE SERVICES (OR ANY FEATURES WITHIN THE SERVICES);

(III) THE DELETION OF, CORRUPTION OF, OR FAILURE TO STORE, ANY CONTENT AND OTHER COMMUNICATIONS DATA MAINTAINED OR TRANSMITTED BY OR THROUGH YOUR USE OF THE SERVICES;

(III) YOUR FAILURE TO PROVIDE GOOGLE WITH ACCURATE ACCOUNT INFORMATION;

(IV) YOUR FAILURE TO KEEP YOUR PASSWORD OR ACCOUNT DETAILS SECURE AND CONFIDENTIAL;

15.2 THE LIMITATIONS ON GOOGLE'S LIABILITY TO YOU IN PARAGRAPH 15.1 ABOVE SHALL APPLY WHETHER OR NOT GOOGLE HAS BEEN ADVISED OF OR SHOULD HAVE BEEN AWARE OF THE POSSIBILITY OF ANY SUCH LOSSES ARISING.

16. Copyright and trade mark policies

16.1 It is Google's policy to respond to notices of alleged copyright infringement that comply with applicable international intellectual property law (including, in the United States, the Digital Millennium Copyright Act) and to terminating the accounts of repeat infringers. Details of Google's policy can be found at http://www.google.com/dmca.html.

16.2 Google operates a trade mark complaints procedure in respect of Google's advertising business, details of which can be found at http://www.google.com/tm_complaint.html.

17. Advertisements

17.1 Some of the Services are supported by advertising revenue and may display advertisements and promotions. These advertisements may be targeted to the content of information stored on the Services, queries made through the Services or other information.

17.2 The manner, mode and extent of advertising by Google on the Services are subject to change without specific notice to you.

17.3 In consideration for Google granting you access to and use of the Services, you agree that Google may place such advertising on the Services.

18. Other content

18.1 The Services may include hyperlinks to other web sites or content or resources. Google may have no control over any web sites or resources which are provided by companies or persons other than Google.

18.2 You acknowledge and agree that Google is not responsible for the availability of any such external sites or resources, and does not endorse any advertising, products or other materials on or available from such web sites or resources.

18.3 You acknowledge and agree that Google is not liable for any loss or damage which may be incurred by you as a result of the availability of those external sites or resources, or as a result of any reliance placed by you on the completeness, accuracy or existence of any advertising, products or other materials on, or available from, such web sites or resources.

19. Changes to the Terms

19.1 Google may make changes to the Universal Terms or Additional Terms from time to time. When these changes are made, Google will make a new copy of the Universal Terms available at http://www.google.com/accounts/TOS?hl=en and any new Additional Terms will be made available to you from within, or through, the affected Services.

19.2 You understand and agree that if you use the Services after the date on which the Universal Terms or Additional Terms have changed, Google will treat your use as acceptance of the updated Universal Terms or Additional Terms.

20. General legal terms

20.1 Sometimes when you use the Services, you may (as a result of, or through your use of the Services) use a service or download a piece of software, or purchase goods, which are provided by another person or company. Your use of these other services, software or goods may be subject to separate terms between you and the company or person concerned. If so, the Terms do not affect your legal relationship with these other companies or individuals.

20.2 The Terms constitute the whole legal agreement between you and Google and govern your use of the Services (but excluding any services which Google may provide to you under a separate written agreement), and completely replace any prior agreements between you and Google in relation to the Services.

20.3 You agree that Google may provide you with notices, including those regarding changes to the Terms, by email, regular mail, or postings on the Services.

20.4 You agree that if Google does not exercise or enforce any legal right or remedy which is contained in the Terms (or which Google has the benefit of under any applicable law), this will not be taken to be a formal waiver of Google's rights and that those rights or remedies will still be available to Google.

20.5 If any court of law, having the jurisdiction to decide on this matter, rules that any provision of these Terms is invalid, then that provision will be removed from the Terms without affecting the rest of the Terms. The remaining provisions of the Terms will continue to be valid and enforceable.

20.6 You acknowledge and agree that each member of the group of companies of which Google is the parent shall be third party beneficiaries to the Terms and that such other companies shall be entitled to directly enforce, and rely upon, any provision of the Terms which confers a benefit on (or rights in favor of) them. Other than this, no other person or company shall be third party beneficiaries to the Terms.

20.7 The Terms, and your relationship with Google under the Terms, shall be governed by the laws of the State of California without regard to its conflict of laws provisions. You and Google agree to submit to the exclusive jurisdiction of the courts located within the county of Santa Clara, California to resolve any legal matter arising from the Terms. Notwithstanding this, you agree that Google shall still be allowed to apply for injunctive remedies (or an equivalent type of urgent legal relief) in any jurisdiction.

April 16, 2007

2008 Google - Home - About Google - Privacy Policy - Terms of Service

YouTube Terms of Service

Community Guidelines

1. Your Acceptance

By using or visiting the YouTube website or any YouTube products, software, data feeds, and services provided to you on, from, or through the YouTube website (collectively the "Service") you signify your agreement to (1) these terms and conditions (the "Terms of Service"), (2) YouTube's privacy notice, found at http://www.youtube.com/t/privacy and incorporated herein by reference, and (3) YouTube's Community Guidelines, found at http://www.youtube.com/t/community_guidelines and also incorporated herein by reference. If you do not agree to any of these terms, the YouTube privacy notice, or the Community Guidelines, please do not use the Service.

Although we may attempt to notify you when major changes are made to these Terms of Service, you should periodically review the most up-to-date version http://www.youtube.com/t/terms). YouTube may, in its sole discretion, modify or revise these Terms of Service and policies at any time, and you agree to be bound by such modifications or revisions. Nothing in these Terms of Service shall be deemed to confer any third-party rights or benefits.

2. Service

These Terms of Service apply to all users of the Service, including users who are also contributors of Content on the Service. "Content" includes the text, software, scripts, graphics, photos, sounds, music, videos, audiovisual combinations, interactive features and other materials you may view on, access through, or contribute to the Service. The Service includes all aspects of YouTube, including but not limited to all products, software and services offered via the YouTube website, such as the YouTube channels, the YouTube "Embeddable Player," the YouTube "Uploader" and other applications.

The Service may contain links to third party websites that are not owned or controlled by YouTube. YouTube has no control over, and assumes no responsibility for, the content, privacy policies, or practices of any third party websites. In addition, YouTube will not and cannot censor or edit the content of any third-party site. By using the Service, you expressly relieve YouTube from any and all liability arising from your use of any third-party website.

Accordingly, we encourage you to be aware when you leave the Service and to read the terms and conditions and privacy policy of each other website that you visit.

3. YouTube Accounts

In order to access some features of the Service, you will have to create a YouTube or Google account. You may never use another's account without permission. When creating your account, you must provide accurate and complete information. You are solely responsible for the activity that occurs on your account, and you must keep your account password secure. You must notify YouTube immediately of any breach of security or unauthorized use of your account.

Although YouTube will not be liable for your losses caused by any unauthorized use of your account, you may be liable for the losses of YouTube or others due to such unauthorized use.

4. General Use of the Service–Permissions and Restrictions

YouTube hereby grants you permission to access and use the Service as set forth in these Terms of Service, provided that:

You agree not to distribute in any medium any part of the Service or the Content without YouTube's prior written authorization, unless YouTube makes available the means for such distribution through functionality offered by the Service (such as the Embeddable Player).

You agree not to alter or modify any part of the Service.

You agree not to access Content through any technology or means other than the video playback pages of the Service itself, the Embeddable Player, or other explicitly authorized means YouTube may designate.

You agree not to use the Service for any of the following commercial uses unless you obtain YouTube's prior written approval:

the sale of access to the Service;

the sale of advertising, sponsorships, or promotions placed on or within the Service or Content; or

the sale of advertising, sponsorships, or promotions on any page of an ad-enabled blog or website containing Content delivered via the Service, unless other material not obtained from YouTube appears on the same page and is of sufficient value to be the basis for such sales.

Prohibited commercial uses do not include:

uploading an original video to YouTube, or maintaining an original channel on YouTube, to promote your business or artistic enterprise;

showing YouTube videos through the Embeddable Player on an ad-enabled blog or website, subject to the advertising restrictions set forth above in Section 4.D; or

any use that YouTube expressly authorizes in writing.

(For more information about what constitutes a prohibited commercial use, see our FAQ.)

If you use the Embeddable Player on your website, you may not modify, build upon, or block any portion or functionality of the Embeddable Player, including but not limited to links back to the YouTube website.

If you use the YouTube Uploader, you agree that it may automatically download and install updates from time to time from YouTube. These updates are designed to improve, enhance and further develop the Uploader and may take the form of bug fixes, enhanced functions, new software modules and completely new versions. You agree to receive such updates (and permit YouTube to deliver these to you) as part of your use of the Uploader.

You agree not to use or launch any automated system, including without limitation, "robots," "spiders," or "offline readers," that accesses the Service in a manner that sends more request messages to the YouTube servers in a given period of time than a human can reasonably produce in the same period by using a conventional on-line web browser. Notwithstanding the foregoing, YouTube grants the operators of public search engines permission to use spiders to copy materials from the site for the sole purpose of and solely to the extent necessary for creating publicly available searchable indices of the materials, but not caches or archives of such materials. YouTube reserves the right to revoke these exceptions either generally or in specific cases. You agree not to collect or harvest any personally identifiable information, including account names, from the Service, nor to use the communication systems provided by the Service (e.g., comments, email) for any commercial solicitation purposes. You agree not to solicit, for commercial purposes, any users of the Service with respect to their Content.

In your use of the Service, you will comply with all applicable laws.

YouTube reserves the right to discontinue any aspect of the Service at any time.

5. Your Use of Content

In addition to the general restrictions above, the following restrictions and conditions apply specifically to your use of Content.

The Content on the Service, and the trademarks, service marks and logos ("Marks") on the Service, are owned by or licensed to YouTube, subject to copyright and other intellectual property rights under the law.

Content is provided to you AS IS. You may access Content for your information and personal use solely as intended through the provided functionality of the Service and as permitted under these Terms of Service. You shall not download any Content unless you see a "download" or similar link displayed by YouTube on the Service for that Content. You shall not copy, reproduce, distribute, transmit, broadcast, display, sell, license, or otherwise exploit any Content for any other purposes without the prior written consent of YouTube or the respective licensors of the Content. YouTube and its licensors reserve all rights not expressly granted in and to the Service and the Content.

You agree not to circumvent, disable or otherwise interfere with security-related features of the Service or features that prevent or restrict use or copying of any Content or enforce limitations on use of the Service or the Content therein.

You understand that when using the Service, you will be exposed to Content from a variety of sources, and that YouTube is not responsible for the accuracy, usefulness, safety, or intellectual property rights of or relating to such Content. You further understand and acknowledge that you may be exposed to Content that is inaccurate, offensive, indecent, or objectionable, and you agree to waive, and hereby do waive, any legal or equitable rights or remedies you have or may have against YouTube with respect thereto, and, to the extent permitted by applicable law, agree to indemnify and hold harmless YouTube, its owners, operators, affiliates, licensors, and licensees to the fullest extent allowed by law regarding all matters related to your use of the Service.

6. Your Content and Conduct

As a YouTube account holder you may submit Content to the Service, including videos and user comments. You understand that YouTube does not guarantee any confidentiality with respect to any Content you submit.

You shall be solely responsible for your own Content and the consequences of submitting and publishing your Content on the Service. You affirm, represent, and warrant that you own or have the necessary licenses, rights, consents, and permissions to publish Content you submit; and you license to YouTube all patent, trademark, trade secret, copyright or other proprietary rights in and to such Content for publication on the Service pursuant to these Terms of Service.

For clarity, you retain all of your ownership rights in your Content. However, by submitting Content to YouTube, you hereby grant YouTube a worldwide, non-exclusive, royalty-free, sublicenseable and transfer-able license to use, reproduce, distribute, prepare derivative works of, display, and perform the Content in connection with the Service and YouTube's (and its successors' and affiliates') business, including without limitation for promoting and redistributing part or all of the Service (and derivative works thereof) in any media formats and through any media channels. You also hereby grant each user of the Service a non-exclusive license to access your Content through the Service, and to use, reproduce, distribute, display and perform such Content as permitted through the functionality of the Service and under these Terms of

Service. The above licenses granted by you in video Content you submit to the Service terminate within a commercially reasonable time after you remove or delete your videos from the Service. You understand and agree, however, that YouTube may retain, but not display, distribute, or perform, server copies of your videos that have been removed or deleted. The above licenses granted by you in user comments you submit are perpetual and irrevocable.

You further agree that Content you submit to the Service will not contain third party copyrighted material, or material that is subject to other third party proprietary rights, unless you have permission from the rightful owner of the material or you are otherwise legally entitled to post the material and to grant YouTube all of the license rights granted herein.

You further agree that you will not submit to the Service any Content or other material that is contrary to the YouTube Community Guidelines, currently found at http://www.youtube.com/t/community_guidelines, which may be updated from time to time, or contrary to applicable local, national, and international laws and regulations.

YouTube does not endorse any Content submitted to the Service by any user or other licensor, or any opinion, recommendation, or advice expressed therein, and YouTube expressly disclaims any and all liability in connection with Content. YouTube does not permit copyright infringing activities and infringement of intellectual property rights on the Service, and YouTube will remove all Content if properly notified that such Content infringes on another's intellectual property rights. YouTube reserves the right to remove Content without prior notice.

7. Account Termination Policy

YouTube will terminate a user's access to the Service if, under appropriate circumstances, the user is determined to be a repeat infringer.

YouTube reserves the right to decide whether Content violates these Terms of Service for reasons other than copyright infringement, such as, but not limited to, pornography, obscenity, or excessive length. YouTube may at any time, without prior notice and in its sole discretion, remove such Content and/or terminate a user's account for submitting such material in violation of these Terms of Service.

8. Digital Millennium Copyright Act

If you are a copyright owner or an agent thereof and believe that any Content infringes upon your copyrights, you may submit a notification pursuant to the Digital Millennium Copyright Act ("DMCA") by providing our Copyright Agent with the following information in writing (see 17 U.S.C 512(c)(3) for further detail):

A physical or electronic signature of a person authorized to act on behalf of the owner of an exclusive right that is allegedly infringed;

Identification of the copyrighted work claimed to have been infringed, or, if multiple copyrighted works at a single online site are covered by a single notification, a representative list of such works at that site;

Identification of the material that is claimed to be infringing or to be the subject of infringing activity and that is to be removed or access to which is to be disabled and information reasonably sufficient to permit the service provider to locate the material;

Information reasonably sufficient to permit the service provider to contact you, such as an address, telephone number, and, if available, an electronic mail;

A statement that you have a good faith belief that use of the material in the manner complained of is not authorized by the copyright owner, its agent, or the law; and

A statement that the information in the notification is accurate, and under penalty of perjury, that you are authorized to act on behalf of the owner of an exclusive right that is allegedly infringed.

YouTube's designated Copyright Agent to receive notifications of claimed infringement is Shadie Farazian, 901 Cherry Ave., San Bruno, CA 94066, email: copyright@youtube.com, fax: 650-872-8513. For clarity, only DMCA notices should go to the Copyright Agent; any other feedback, comments, requests for technical support, and other communications should be directed to YouTube customer service through http://www.google.com/support/youtube. You acknowledge that if you fail to comply with all of the requirements of this Section 5(D), your DMCA notice may not be valid.

Counter-Notice. If you believe that your Content that was removed (or to which access was disabled) is not infringing, or that you have the authorization from the copyright owner, the copyright owner's agent, or pursuant to the law, to post and use the material in your Content, you may send a counter-notice containing the following information to the Copyright Agent:

Your physical or electronic signature;

Identification of the Content that has been removed or to which access has been disabled and the location at which the Content appeared before it was removed or disabled;

A statement that you have a good faith belief that the Content was removed or disabled as a result of mistake or a misidentification of the Content; and

Your name, address, telephone number, and e-mail address, a statement that you consent to the jurisdiction of the federal court in San Francisco, California, and a statement that you will accept service of process from the person who provided notification of the alleged infringement.

If a counter-notice is received by the Copyright Agent, YouTube may send a copy of the counter-notice to the original complaining party informing that person that it may replace the removed Content or cease disabling it in 10 business days. Unless the copyright owner files an action seeking a court order against the Content provider, member or user, the removed Content may be replaced, or access to it restored, in 10 to 14 business days or more after receipt of the counter-notice, at YouTube's sole discretion.

9. Warranty Disclaimer

YOU AGREE THAT YOUR USE OF THE SERVICES SHALL BE AT YOUR SOLE RISK. TO THE FULLEST EXTENT PERMITTED BY LAW, YOUTUBE, ITS OFFICERS, DIRECTORS, EMPLOYEES, AND AGENTS DISCLAIM ALL WARRANTIES, EXPRESS OR IMPLIED, IN CONNECTION WITH THE SERVICES AND YOUR USE THEREOF. YOUTUBE MAKES NO WARRANTIES OR REPRESENTATIONS ABOUT THE ACCURACY OR COMPLETENESS OF THIS SITE'S CONTENT OR THE CONTENT OF ANY SITES LINKED TO THIS SITE AND ASSUMES NO LIABILITY OR RESPONSIBILITY FOR ANY (I) ERRORS, MISTAKES, OR INACCURACIES OF CONTENT, (II) PERSONAL INJURY OR PROPERTY DAMAGE, OF ANY NATURE WHATSOEVER, RESULTING FROM YOUR ACCESS TO AND USE OF OUR SERVICES, (III) ANY UNAUTHORIZED ACCESS TO OR USE OF OUR SECURE SERVERS AND/OR ANY AND ALL PERSONAL INFORMATION AND/OR FINANCIAL INFORMATION STORED THEREIN, (IV) ANY INTERRUPTION OR CESSATION OF TRANSMISSION TO OR FROM OUR SERVICES, (IV) ANY BUGS, VIRUSES, TROJAN HORSES, OR THE LIKE WHICH MAY BE TRANSMITTED TO OR THROUGH OUR SERVICES BY ANY THIRD PARTY, AND/OR (V) ANY ERRORS OR OMISSIONS IN ANY CONTENT OR FOR ANY LOSS OR DAMAGE OF ANY KIND INCURRED AS A RESULT OF THE USE OF ANY CONTENT POSTED, EMAILED, TRANSMITTED, OR OTHERWISE MADE AVAILABLE VIA THE SERVICES. YOUTUBE DOES NOT WARRANT, ENDORSE, GUARANTEE, OR ASSUME RESPONSIBILITY FOR ANY PRODUCT OR SERVICE ADVERTISED OR OFFERED BY A THIRD PARTY THROUGH THE SERVICES OR ANY HYPERLINKED SERVICES OR FEATURED IN ANY BANNER OR OTHER ADVERTISING, AND YOUTUBE WILL NOT BE A PARTY TO OR IN ANY WAY BE RESPONSIBLE FOR MONITORING ANY TRANSACTION BETWEEN YOU AND THIRD-PARTY PROVIDERS OF PRODUCTS OR SERVICES. AS WITH THE PURCHASE OF A PRODUCT OR SERVICE THROUGH ANY MEDIUM OR IN ANY ENVIRONMENT, YOU SHOULD USE YOUR BEST JUDGMENT AND EXERCISE CAUTION WHERE APPROPRIATE.

10. Limitation of Liability

IN NO EVENT SHALL YOUTUBE, ITS OFFICERS, DIRECTORS, EMPLOYEES, OR AGENTS, BE LIABLE TO YOU FOR ANY DIRECT, INDIRECT, INCIDENTAL, SPECIAL, PUNITIVE, OR CONSEQUENTIAL DAMAGES WHATSOEVER RESULTING FROM ANY (I) ERRORS, MISTAKES, OR INACCURACIES OF

CONTENT, (II) PERSONAL INJURY OR PROPERTY DAMAGE, OF ANY NATURE WHATSOEVER, RESULTING FROM YOUR ACCESS TO AND USE OF OUR SERVICES, (III) ANY UNAUTHORIZED ACCESS TO OR USE OF OUR SECURE SERVERS AND/OR ANY AND ALL PERSONAL INFORMATION AND/OR FINANCIAL INFORMATION STORED THEREIN, (IV) ANY INTERRUPTION OR CESSATION OF TRANS-MISSION TO OR FROM OUR SERVICES, (IV) ANY BUGS, VIRUSES, TROJAN HORSES, OR THE LIKE, WHICH MAY BE TRANSMITTED TO OR THROUGH OUR SERVICES BY ANY THIRD PARTY, AND/OR (V) ANY ERRORS OR OMISSIONS IN ANY CONTENT OR FOR ANY LOSS OR DAMAGE OF ANY KIND INCURRED AS A RESULT OF YOUR USE OF ANY CONTENT POSTED, EMAILED, TRANSMITTED, OR OTHERWISE MADE AVAILABLE VIA THE SERVICES, WHETHER BASED ON WARRANTY, CONTRACT, TORT, OR ANY OTHER LEGAL THEORY, AND WHETHER OR NOT THE COMPANY IS ADVISED OF THE POSSIBILITY OF SUCH DAMAGES. THE FOREGOING LIMITATION OF LIABILITY SHALL APPLY TO THE FULLEST EXTENT PERMITTED BY LAW IN THE APPLICABLE JURISDICTION.
YOU SPECIFICALLY ACKNOWLEDGE THAT YOUTUBE SHALL NOT BE LIABLE FOR CONTENT OR THE DEFAMATORY, OFFENSIVE, OR ILLEGAL CONDUCT OF ANY THIRD PARTY AND THAT THE RISK OF HARM OR DAMAGE FROM THE FOREGOING RESTS ENTIRELY WITH YOU.

The Service is controlled and offered by YouTube from its facilities in the United States of America. YouTube makes no representations that the Service is appropriate or available for use in other locations. Those who access or use the Service from other jurisdictions do so at their own volition and are responsible for compliance with local law.

11. Indemnity

To the extent permitted by applicable law, you agree to defend, indemnify and hold harmless YouTube, its parent corporation, officers, directors, employees and agents, from and against any and all claims, damages, obligations, losses, liabilities, costs or debt, and expenses (including but not limited to attorney's fees) arising from: (i) your use of and access to the Service; (ii) your violation of any term of these Terms of Service; (iii) your violation of any third party right, including without limitation any copyright, property, or privacy right; or (iv) any claim that your Content caused damage to a third party. This defense and indemnification obligation will survive these Terms of Service and your use of the Service.

12. Ability to Accept Terms of Service

You affirm that you are either more than 18 years of age, or an emancipated minor, or possess legal parental or guardian consent, and are fully able and competent to enter into the terms, conditions, obligations, affirmations, representations, and warranties set forth in these Terms of Service, and to abide by and comply with these Terms of Service. In any case, you affirm that you are over the age of 13, as the Service is not intended for children under 13. If you are under 13 years of age, then please do not use the Service. There are lots of other great web sites for you. Talk to your parents about what sites are appropriate for you.

13. Assignment

These Terms of Service, and any rights and licenses granted hereunder, may not be transferred or assigned by you, but may be assigned by YouTube without restriction.

14. General

You agree that: (i) the Service shall be deemed solely based in California; and (ii) the Service shall be deemed a passive website that does not give rise to personal jurisdiction over YouTube, either specific or general, in jurisdictions other than California. These Terms of Service shall be governed by the internal substantive laws of the State of California, without respect to its conflict of laws principles. Any claim or dispute between you and YouTube that arises in whole or in part from the Service shall be decided exclusively by a court of competent jurisdiction located in Santa Clara County, California. These Terms of Service, together with the Privacy Notice at http://www.youtube.com/t/privacy and any other legal notices published by YouTube on the Service, shall constitute the entire agreement between you and

YouTube concerning the Service. If any provision of these Terms of Service is deemed invalid by a court of competent jurisdiction, the invalidity of such provision shall not affect the validity of the remaining provisions of these Terms of Service, which shall remain in full force and effect. No waiver of any term of this these Terms of Service shall be deemed a further or continuing waiver of such term or any other term, and YouTube's failure to assert any right or provision under these Terms of Service shall not constitute a waiver of such right or provision. YouTube reserves the right to amend these Terms of Service at any time and without notice, and it is your responsibility to review these Terms of Service for any changes. Your use of the Service following any amendment of these Terms of Service will signify your assent to and acceptance of its revised terms. YOU AND YOUTUBE AGREE THAT ANY CAUSE OF ACTION ARISING OUT OF OR RELATED TO THE SERVICES MUST COMMENCE WITHIN ONE (1) YEAR AFTER THE CAUSE OF ACTION ACCRUES. OTHERWISE, SUCH CAUSE OF ACTION IS PERMANENTLY BARRED.

Dated: June 9, 2010

Twitter Terms of Service

These Terms of Service ("**Terms**") govern your access to and use of the services and Twitter's websites (the "**Services**"), and any information, text, graphics, or other materials uploaded, downloaded or appearing on the Services (collectively referred to as "**Content**"). Your access to and use of the Services is conditioned on your acceptance of and compliance with these Terms. By accessing or using the Services you agree to be bound by these Terms.

Basic Terms

You are responsible for your use of the Services, for any content you post to the Services, and for any consequences thereof. The Content you submit, post, or display will be able to be viewed by other users of the Services and through third party services and websites (go to the account settings page to control who sees your Content). You should only provide Content that you are comfortable sharing with others under these Terms.

Tip What you say on Twitter may be viewed all around the world instantly. You are what you Tweet!

You may use the Services only if you can form a binding contract with Twitter and are not a person barred from receiving services under the laws of the United States or other applicable jurisdiction. You may use the Services only in compliance with these Terms and all applicable local, state, national, and international laws, rules and regulations.

The Services that Twitter provides are always evolving and the form and nature of the Services that Twitter provides may change from time to time without prior notice to you. In addition, Twitter may stop (permanently or temporarily) providing the Services (or any features within the Services) to you or to users generally and may not be able to provide you with prior notice. We also retain the right to create limits on use and storage at our sole discretion at any time without prior notice to you.

The Services may include advertisements, which may be targeted to the Content or information on the Services, queries made through the Services, or other information. The types and extent of advertising by Twitter on the Services are subject to change. In consideration for Twitter granting you access to and use of the Services, you agree that Twitter and its third party providers and partners may place such advertising on the Services or in connection with the display of Content or information from the Services whether submitted by you or others.

Privacy

Any information that you provide to Twitter is subject to our Privacy Policy, which governs our collection and use of your information. You understand that through your use of the Services you consent to the collection and use (as set forth in the Privacy Policy) of this information, including the transfer of this information to the United States and/or other countries for storage, processing and use by Twitter. As part of providing you the Services, we may need to provide you with certain communications, such as service announcements and administrative messages. These communications are considered part of the Services and your Twitter account, which you may not be able to opt-out from receiving.

Tip You can opt-out of most communications from Twitter including our newsletter, new follower emails, etc. Please see the Notifications tab of Settings for more.

Passwords

You are responsible for safeguarding the password that you use to access the Services and for any activities or actions under your password. We encourage you to use "strong" passwords (passwords that use a combination of upper and lower case letters, numbers and symbols) with your account. Twitter cannot and will not be liable for any loss or damage arising from your failure to comply with the above requirements.

Content on the Services

All Content, whether publicly posted or privately transmitted, is the sole responsibility of the person who originated such Content. We may not monitor or control the Content posted via the Services and, we cannot take responsibility for such Content. Any use or reliance on any Content or materials posted via the Services or obtained by you through the Services is at your own risk.

We do not endorse, support, represent or guarantee the completeness, truthfulness, accuracy, or reliability of any Content or communications posted via the Services or endorse any opinions expressed via the Services. You understand that by using the Services, you may be exposed to Content that might be offensive, harmful, inaccurate or otherwise inappropriate, or in some cases, postings that have been mislabeled or are otherwise deceptive. Under no circumstances will Twitter be liable in any way for any Content, including, but not limited to, any errors or omissions in any Content, or any loss or damage of any kind incurred as a result of the use of any Content posted, emailed, transmitted or otherwise made available via the Services or broadcast elsewhere.

Your Rights

You retain your rights to any Content you submit, post or display on or through the Services. By submitting, posting or displaying Content on or through the Services, you grant us a worldwide, non-exclusive, royalty-free license (with the right to sublicense) to use, copy, reproduce, process, adapt, modify, publish, transmit, display and distribute such Content in any and all media or distribution methods (now known or later developed).

Tip This license is you authorizing us to make your Tweets available to the rest of the world and to let others do the same. But what's yours is yours – you own your content.

You agree that this license includes the right for Twitter to make such Content available to other companies, organizations or individuals who partner with Twitter for the syndication, broadcast, distribution or publication of such Content on other media and services, subject to our terms and conditions for such Content use.

Tip Twitter has an evolving set of rules for how API developers can interact with your content. These rules exist to enable an open ecosystem with your rights in mind.
Such additional uses by Twitter, or other companies, organizations or individuals who partner with Twitter, may be made with no compensation paid to you with respect to the Content that you submit, post, transmit or otherwise make available through the Services.

We may modify or adapt your Content in order to transmit, display or distribute it over computer networks and in various media and/or make changes to your Content as are necessary to conform and adapt that Content to any requirements or limitations of any networks, devices, services or media.

You are responsible for your use of the Services, for any Content you provide, and for any consequences thereof, including the use of your Content by other users and our third party partners. You understand that your Content may be rebroadcasted by our partners and if you do not have the right to submit Content for such use, it may subject you to liability. Twitter will not be responsible or liable for any use of your Content by Twitter in accordance with these Terms. You represent and warrant that you have all the rights, power and authority necessary to grant the rights granted herein to any Content that you submit.

Twitter gives you a personal, worldwide, royalty-free, non-assignable and non-exclusive license to use the software that is provided to you by Twitter as part of the Services. This license is for the sole purpose of enabling you to use and enjoy the benefit of the Services as provided by Twitter, in the manner permitted by these Terms.

Twitter Rights
All right, title, and interest in and to the Services (excluding Content provided by users) are and will remain the exclusive property of Twitter and its licensors. The Services are protected by copyright, trademark, and other laws of both the United States and foreign countries. Nothing in the Terms gives you a right to use the Twitter name or any of the Twitter trademarks, logos, domain names, and other distinctive brand features. Any feedback, comments, or suggestions you may provide regarding Twitter, or the Services is entirely voluntary and we will be free to use such feedback, comments or suggestions as we see fit and without any obligation to you.

Restrictions on Content and Use of the Services
We reserve the right at all times (but will not have an obligation) to remove or refuse to distribute any Content on the Services and to terminate users or reclaim usernames. Please review the Twitter Rules (which are part of these Terms) to better understand what is prohibited on the Service. We also reserve the right to access, read, preserve, and disclose any information as we reasonably believe is necessary to (i) satisfy any applicable law, regulation, legal process or governmental request, (ii) enforce the Terms, including investigation of potential violations hereof, (iii) detect, prevent, or otherwise address fraud, security or technical issues, (iv) respond to user support requests, or (v) protect the rights, property or safety of Twitter, its users and the public.

Tip Twitter does not disclose personally identifying information to third parties except in accordance with our Privacy Policy.

Except as permitted through the Services (or these Terms), you have to use the Twitter API if you want to reproduce, modify, create derivative works, distribute, sell, transfer, publicly display, publicly perform, transmit, or otherwise use the Content or Services.

Tip We encourage and permit broad re-use of Content. The Twitter API exists to enable this.

You may not do any of the following while accessing or using the Services: (i) access, tamper with, or use non-public areas of the Services, Twitter's computer systems, or the technical delivery systems of Twitter's providers; (ii) probe, scan, or test the vulnerability of any system or network or breach or circumvent any security or authentication measures; (iii) access or search or attempt to access or search the Services by any means (automated or otherwise) other than through our currently available, published interfaces that are provided by Twitter (and only pursuant to those terms and conditions), unless you have been specifically allowed to do so in a separate agreement with Twitter (NOTE: crawling the Services is permissible if done in accordance with the provisions of the robots.txt file, however, scraping the Services without the prior consent of Twitter is expressly prohibited); (iv) forge any TCP/IP packet header or any part of the header information in any email or posting, or in any way use the Services to send altered, deceptive or false source-identifying information; or (v) interfere with, or disrupt, (or attempt to do so), the access of any user, host or network, including, without limitation, sending a virus, overloading, flooding, spamming, mail-bombing the Services, or by scripting the creation of Content in such a manner as to interfere with or create an undue burden on the Services.

Copyright Policy

Twitter respects the intellectual property rights of others and expects users of the Services to do the same. We will respond to notices of alleged copyright infringement that comply with applicable law and are properly provided to us. If you believe that your Content has been copied in a way that constitutes copyright infringement, please provide us with the following information: (i) a physical or electronic signature of the copyright owner or a person authorized to act on their behalf; (ii) identification of the copyrighted work claimed to have been infringed; (iii) identification of the material that is claimed to be infringing or to be the subject of infringing activity and that is to be removed or access to which is to be disabled, and information reasonably sufficient to permit us to locate the material; (iv) your contact information, including your address, telephone number, and an email address; (v) a statement by you that you have a good faith belief that use of the material in the manner complained of is not authorized by the copyright owner, its agent, or the law; and (vi) a statement that the information in the notification is accurate, and, under penalty of perjury, that you are authorized to act on behalf of the copyright owner.

We reserve the right to remove Content alleged to be infringing without prior notice and at our sole discretion. In appropriate circumstances, Twitter will also terminate a user's account if the user is determined to be a repeat infringer. Our designated copyright agent for notice of alleged copyright infringement appearing on the Services is:
Twitter, Inc.
Attn: Copyright Agent
795 Folsom Street, Suite 600
San Francisco, CA 94107
Email: copyright@twitter.com

The Services are Available "AS-IS"

Your access to and use of the Services or any Content is at your own risk. You understand and agree that the Services is provided to you on an "AS IS" and "AS AVAILABLE" basis. Without limiting the foregoing, TWITTER AND ITS PARTNERS DISCLAIM ANY WARRANTIES, EXPRESS OR IMPLIED, OF MERCHANT-ABILITY, FITNESS FOR A PARTICULAR PURPOSE, OR NON-INFRINGEMENT. We make no warranty and disclaim all responsibility and liability for the completeness, accuracy, availability, timeliness, security or reliability of the Services or any content thereon. Twitter will not be responsible or liable for any harm to your computer system, loss of data, or other harm that results from your access to or use of the Services, or any Content. You also agree that Twitter has no responsibility or liability for the deletion of, or the failure to store or to transmit, any Content and other communications maintained by the Services. We make no warranty that the Services will meet your requirements or be available on an uninterrupted, secure, or error-free basis. No advice or information, whether oral or written, obtained from Twitter or through the Services, will create any warranty not expressly made herein.

Links

The Services may contain links to third-party websites or resources. You acknowledge and agree that we are not responsible or liable for: (i) the availability or accuracy of such websites or resources; or (ii) the content, products, or services on or available from such websites or resources. Links to such websites or resources do not imply any endorsement by Twitter of such websites or resources or the content, products, or services available from such websites or resources. You acknowledge sole responsibility for and assume all risk arising from your use of any such websites or resources.

Limitation of Liability

TO THE MAXIMUM EXTENT PERMITTED BY APPLICABLE LAW, TWITTER AND ITS SUBSIDIARIES, AFFILIATES, OFFICERS, EMPLOYEES, AGENTS, PARTNERS AND LICENSORS WILL NOT BE LIABLE FOR ANY DIRECT, INDIRECT, INCIDENTAL, SPECIAL, CONSEQUENTIAL OR PUNITIVE DAMAGES, INCLUD-ING WITHOUT LIMITATION, LOSS OF PROFITS, DATA, USE, GOOD-WILL, OR OTHER INTANGIBLE LOSSES, RESULTING FROM (i) YOUR ACCESS TO OR USE OF OR INABILITY TO ACCESS OR USE THE SERVICES; (ii) ANY CONDUCT OR CONTENT OF ANY THIRD PARTY ON THE SERVICES, INCLUDING WITHOUT LIMITATION, ANY DEFAMATORY, OFFENSIVE OR ILLEGAL CONDUCT OF OTHER USERS OR THIRD PARTIES; (iii) ANY CONTENT OBTAINED FROM THE SERVICES; AND (iv) UNAUTHORIZED ACCESS, USE OR ALTERATION OF YOUR TRANSMISSIONS OR CONTENT, WHETHER BASED ON WARRANTY, CONTRACT, TORT (INCLUDING NEGLIGENCE) OR ANY OTHER LEGAL THEORY, WHETHER OR NOT TWITTER HAS BEEN INFORMED OF THE POSSIBILITY OF SUCH DAMAGE, AND EVEN IF A REMEDY SET FORTH HEREIN IS FOUND TO HAVE FAILED OF ITS ESSENTIAL PURPOSE.

Exclusions

Some jurisdictions do not allow the exclusion of certain warranties or the exclusion or limitation of liability for consequential or incidental damages, so the limitations above may not apply to you.

Waiver and Severability

The failure of Twitter to enforce any right or provision of these Terms will not be deemed a waiver of such right or provision. In the event that any provision of these Terms is held to be invalid or unenforceable, the remaining provisions of these Terms will remain in full force and effect.

Controlling Law and Jurisdiction

These Terms and any action related thereto will be governed by the laws of the State of California without regard to or application of its conflict of law provisions or your state or country of residence. All claims, legal proceedings or litigation arising in connection with the Services will be brought solely in San Francisco County, California, and you consent to the jurisdiction of and venue in such courts and waive any objection as to inconvenient forum. If you are accepting these Terms on behalf of a United States federal government entity that is legally unable to accept the controlling law, jurisdiction or venue clauses above, then those clauses do not apply to you but instead these Terms and any action related thereto will be will be governed by the laws of the United States of America (without reference to conflict of laws) and, in the absence of federal law and to the extent permitted under federal law, the laws of the State of California (excluding choice of law).

Entire Agreement

These Terms, the Twitter Rules and our Privacy Policy are the entire and exclusive agreement between Twitter and you regarding the Services (excluding any services for which you have a separate agreement with Twitter that is explicitly in addition or in place of these Terms), and these Terms supersede and replace any prior agreements between Twitter and you regarding the Services. Other than members of the group of companies of which Twitter is the parent, no other person or company will be third party beneficiaries to the Terms.

We may revise these Terms from time to time, the most current version will always be at twitter.com/tos. If the revision, in our sole discretion, is material we will notify you via an @Twitter update or e-mail to the email associated with your account. By continuing to access or use the Services after those revisions become effective, you agree to be bound by the revised Terms.

These Services are operated and provided by Twitter Inc., 795 Folsom Street, Suite 600, San Francisco, CA 94107. If you have any questions about these Terms, please contact us.
Effective: November 16, 2010

Archive of Previous Terms

---

facebook

This agreement was written in English (US). To the extent any translated version of this agreement conflicts with the English version, the English version controls. Please note that Section 16 contains certain changes to the general terms for users outside the United States.
Date of Last Revision: October 4, 2010.

Statement of Rights and Responsibilities

This Statement of Rights and Responsibilities ("Statement") derives from the Facebook Principles, and governs our relationship with users and others who interact with Facebook. By using or accessing Facebook, you agree to this Statement.

1.   **Privacy**

      Your privacy is very important to us. We designed our Privacy Policy to make important disclosures about how you can use Facebook to share with others and how we collect and can use your content and information. We encourage you to read the Privacy Policy, and to use it to help make informed decisions.

2. Sharing Your Content and Information

You own all of the content and information you post on Facebook, and you can control how it is shared through your privacy and application settings. In addition:

1. For content that is covered by intellectual property rights, like photos and videos ("IP content"), you specifically give us the following permission, subject to your privacy and application settings: you grant us a non-exclusive, transferable, sub-licensable, royalty-free, worldwide license to use any IP content that you post on or in connection with Facebook ("IP License"). This IP License ends when you delete your IP content or your account unless your content has been shared with others, and they have not deleted it.

2. When you delete IP content, it is deleted in a manner similar to emptying the recycle bin on a computer. However, you understand that removed content may persist in backup copies for a reasonable period of time (but will not be available to others).

3. When you use an application, your content and information is shared with the application. We require applications to respect your privacy, and your agreement with that application will control how the application can use, store, and transfer that content and information. (To learn more about Platform, read our Privacy Policy and Platform Page.)

4. When you publish content or information using the "everyone" setting, it means that you are allowing everyone, including people off of Facebook, to access and use that information, and to associate it with you (i.e., your name and profile picture).

5. We always appreciate your feedback or other suggestions about Facebook, but you understand that we may use them without any obligation to compensate you for them (just as you have no obligation to offer them).

3. Safety

We do our best to keep Facebook safe, but we cannot guarantee it. We need your help to do that, which includes the following commitments:

1. You will not send or otherwise post unauthorized commercial communications (such as spam) on Facebook.

2. You will not collect users' content or information, or otherwise access Facebook, using automated means (such as harvesting bots, robots, spiders, or scrapers) without our permission.

3. You will not engage in unlawful multi-level marketing, such as a pyramid scheme, on Facebook.

4. You will not upload viruses or other malicious code.

5. You will not solicit login information or access an account belonging to someone else.

6. You will not bully, intimidate, or harass any user.

7. You will not post content that: is hateful, threatening, or pornographic; incites violence; or contains nudity or graphic or gratuitous violence.

8. You will not develop or operate a third-party application containing alcohol-related or other mature content (including advertisements) without appropriate age-based restrictions.

9. You will not offer any contest, giveaway, or sweepstakes ("promotion") on Facebook without our prior written consent. If we consent, you take full responsibility for the promotion, and will follow our Promotions Guidelines and all applicable laws.
10. You will not use Facebook to do anything unlawful, misleading, malicious, or discriminatory.
11. You will not do anything that could disable, overburden, or impair the proper working of Facebook, such as a denial of service attack.
12. You will not facilitate or encourage any violations of this Statement.

4. Registration and Account Security

Facebook users provide their real names and information, and we need your help to keep it that way. Here are some commitments you make to us relating to registering and maintaining the security of your account:

1. You will not provide any false personal information on Facebook, or create an account for anyone other than yourself without permission.
2. You will not create more than one personal profile.
3. If we disable your account, you will not create another one without our permission.
4. You will not use your personal profile for your own commercial gain (such as selling your status update to an advertiser).
5. You will not use Facebook if you are under 13.
6. You will not use Facebook if you are a convicted sex offender.
7. You will keep your contact information accurate and up-to-date.
8. You will not share your password, (or in the case of developers, your secret key), let anyone else access your account, or do anything else that might jeopardize the security of your account.
9. You will not transfer your account (including any page or application you administer) to anyone without first getting our written permission.
10. If you select a username for your account we reserve the right to remove or reclaim it if we believe appropriate (such as when a trademark owner complains about a username that does not closely relate to a user's actual name).

5. Protecting Other People's Rights

We respect other people's rights, and expect you to do the same.

1. You will not post content or take any action on Facebook that infringes or violates someone else's rights or otherwise violates the law.
2. We can remove any content or information you post on Facebook if we believe that it violates this Statement.
3. We will provide you with tools to help you protect your intellectual property rights. To learn more, visit our How to Report Claims of Intellectual Property Infringement page.
4. If we remove your content for infringing someone else's copyright, and you believe we removed it by mistake, we will provide you with an opportunity to appeal.
5. If you repeatedly infringe other people's intellectual property rights, we will disable your account when appropriate.
6. You will not use our copyrights or trademarks (including Facebook, the Facebook and F Logos, FB, Face, Poke, Wall and 32665), or any confusingly similar marks, without our written permission.
7. If you collect information from users, you will: obtain their consent, make it clear you

(and not Facebook) are the one collecting their information, and post a privacy policy explaining what information you collect and how you will use it.

8. You will not post anyone's identification documents or sensitive financial information on Facebook.

9. You will not tag users or send email invitations to non-users without their consent.

6. Mobile

1. We currently provide our mobile services for free, but please be aware that your carrier's normal rates and fees, such as text messaging fees, will still apply.

2. In the event you change or deactivate your mobile telephone number, you will update your account information on Facebook within 48 hours to ensure that your messages are not sent to the person who acquires your old number.

3. You provide all rights necessary to enable users to sync (including through an application) their contact lists with any basic information and contact information that is visible to them on Facebook, as well as your name and profile picture.

7. Payments and Deals

1. If you make a payment on Facebook or use Facebook Credits, you agree to our Payments Terms.

2. If purchase a Deal, you agree to our Deals Terms.

3. If you provide a Deal or partner with us to provide a Deal, you agree to the Merchant Deal Terms in addition to any other agreements you may have with us.

8. Special Provisions Applicable to Share Links

If you include our Share Link button on your website, the following additional terms apply to you:

1. We give you permission to use Facebook's Share Link button so that users can post links or content from your website on Facebook.

2. You give us permission to use and allow others to use such links and content on Facebook.

3. You will not place a Share Link button on any page containing content that would violate this Statement if posted on Facebook.

9. Special Provisions Applicable to Developers/Operators of Applications and Websites

If you are a developer or operator of a Platform application or website, the following additional terms apply to you:

1. You are responsible for your application and its content and all uses you make of Platform. This includes ensuring your application or use of Platform meets our Facebook Platform Policies and our Advertising Guidelines.

2. Your access to and use of data you receive from Facebook, will be limited as follows:

    1. You will only request data you need to operate your application.

    2. You will have a privacy policy that tells users what user data you are going to use and how you will use, display, share, or transfer that data and you will include your privacy policy URL in the Developer Application.

    3. You will not use, display, share, or transfer a user's data in a manner inconsistent with your privacy policy.

4. You will delete all data you receive from us concerning a user if the user asks you to do so, and will provide a mechanism for users to make such a request.
5. You will not include data you receive from us concerning a user in any advertising creative.
6. You will not directly or indirectly transfer any data you receive from us to (or use such data in connection with) any ad network, ad exchange, data broker, or other advertising related toolset, even if a user consents to that transfer or use.
7. You will not sell user data. If you are acquired by or merge with a third party, you can continue to use user data within your application, but you cannot transfer user data outside of your application.
8. We can require you to delete user data if you use it in a way that we determine is inconsistent with users' expectations.
9. We can limit your access to data.
10. You will comply with all other restrictions contained in our Facebook Platform Policies.
3. You will not give us information that you independently collect from a user or a user's content without that user's consent.
4. You will make it easy for users to remove or disconnect from your application.
5. You will make it easy for users to contact you. We can also share your email address with users and others claiming that you have infringed or otherwise violated their rights.
6. You will provide customer support for your application.
7. You will not show third party ads or web search boxes on Facebook.
8. We give you all rights necessary to use the code, APIs, data, and tools you receive from us.
9. You will not sell, transfer, or sublicense our code, APIs, or tools to anyone.
10. You will not misrepresent your relationship with Facebook to others.
11. You may use the logos we make available to developers or issue a press release or other public statement so long as you follow our Facebook Platform Policies.
12. We can issue a press release describing our relationship with you.
13. You will comply with all applicable laws. In particular you will (if applicable):
    1. have a policy for removing infringing content and terminating repeat infringers that complies with the Digital Millennium Copyright Act.
    2. comply with the Video Privacy Protection Act ("VPPA"), and obtain any opt-in consent necessary from users so that user data subject to the VPPA may be shared on Facebook. You represent that any disclosure to us will not be incidental to the ordinary course of your business.
14. We do not guarantee that Platform will always be free.
15. You give us all rights necessary to enable your application to work with Facebook, including the right to incorporate content and information you provide to us into streams, profiles, and user action stories.
16. You give us the right to link to or frame your application, and place content, including ads, around your application.
17. We can analyze your application, content, and data for any purpose, including

commercial (such as for targeting the delivery of advertisements and indexing content for search).

18. To ensure your application is safe for users, we can audit it.

19. We can create applications that offer similar features and services to, or otherwise compete with, your application.

10. About Advertisements and Other Commercial Content Served or Enhanced by Facebook

Our goal is to deliver ads that are not only valuable to advertisers, but also valuable to you. In order to do that, you agree to the following:

1. You can use your privacy settings to limit how your name and profile picture may be associated with commercial, sponsored, or related content (such as a brand you like) served or enhanced by us. You give us permission to use your name and profile picture in connection with that content, subject to the limits you place.

2. We do not give your content or information to advertisers without your consent.

3. You understand that we may not always identify paid services and communications as such.

11. Special Provisions Applicable to Advertisers

You can target your specific audience by buying ads on Facebook or our publisher network. The following additional terms apply to you if you place an order through our online advertising portal ("Order"):

1. When you place an Order, you will tell us the type of advertising you want to buy, the amount you want to spend, and your bid. If we accept your Order, we will deliver your ads as inventory becomes available. When serving your ad, we do our best to deliver the ads to the audience you specify, although we cannot guarantee in every instance that your ad will reach its intended target.

2. In instances where we believe doing so will enhance the effectiveness of your advertising campaign, we may broaden the targeting criteria you specify.

3. You will pay for your Orders in accordance with our Payments Terms. The amount you owe will be calculated based on our tracking mechanisms.

4. Your ads will comply with our Advertising Guidelines.

5. We will determine the size, placement, and positioning of your ads.

6. We do not guarantee the activity that your ads will receive, such as the number of clicks you will get.

7. We cannot control how people interact with your ads, and are not responsible for click fraud or other improper actions that affect the cost of running ads. We do, however, have systems to detect and filter certain suspicious activity, learn more here.

8. You can cancel your Order at any time through our online portal, but it may take up to 24 hours before the ad stops running. You are responsible for paying for those ads.

9. Our license to run your ad will end when we have completed your Order. You understand, however, that if users have interacted with your ad, your ad may remain until the users delete it.

10. We can use your ads and related content and information for marketing or promotional purposes.

11. You will not issue any press release or make public statements about your relationship with Facebook without written permission.

12. We may reject or remove any ad for any reason.
13. If you are placing ads on someone else's behalf, we need to make sure you have permission to place those ads, including the following:
    1. You warrant that you have the legal authority to bind the advertiser to this Statement.
    2. You agree that if the advertiser you represent violates this Statement, we may hold you responsible for that violation.

12. Special Provisions Applicable to Pages

If you create or administer a Page on Facebook, you agree to our Pages Terms.

13. Amendments

1. We can change this Statement if we provide you notice (by posting the change on the Facebook Site Governance Page) and an opportunity to comment. To get notice of any future changes to this Statement, visit our Facebook Site Governance Page and become a fan.
2. For changes to sections 7, 8, 9, and 11 (sections relating to payments, application developers, website operators, and advertisers), we will give you a minimum of three days' notice. For all other changes we will give you a minimum of seven days notice. All such comments must be made on the Facebook Site Governance Page.
3. If more than 7,000 users comment on the proposed change, we will also give you the opportunity to participate in a vote in which you will be provided alternatives. The vote shall be binding on us if more than 30 percent of all active registered users as of the date of the notice vote.
4. We can make changes for legal or administrative reasons, or to correct an inaccurate statement, upon notice without opportunity to comment.

14. Termination

If you violate the letter or spirit of this Statement, or otherwise create risk or possible legal exposure for us, we can stop providing all or part of Facebook to you. We will notify you by email or at the next time you attempt to access your account. You may also delete your account or disable your application at any time. In all such cases, this Statement shall terminate, but the following provisions will still apply: 2.2, 2.4, 3-5, 8.2, 9.1-9.3, 9.9, 9.10, 9.13, 9.15, 9.18, 10.3, 11.2, 11.5, 11.6, 11.9, 11.12, 11.13, and 14-18.

15. Disputes

1. You will resolve any claim, cause of action or dispute ("claim") you have with us arising out of or relating to this Statement or Facebook exclusively in a state or federal court located in Santa Clara County. The laws of the State of California will govern this Statement, as well as any claim that might arise between you and us, without regard to conflict of law provisions. You agree to submit to the personal jurisdiction of the courts located in Santa Clara County, California for the purpose of litigating all such claims.
2. If anyone brings a claim against us related to your actions, content or information on Facebook, you will indemnify and hold us harmless from and against all damages, losses, and expenses of any kind (including reasonable legal fees and costs) related to such claim.

3. WE TRY TO KEEP FACEBOOK UP, BUG-FREE, AND SAFE, BUT YOU USE IT AT YOUR OWN RISK. WE ARE PROVIDING FACEBOOK "AS IS" WITHOUT ANY EXPRESS OR IMPLIED WARRANTIES INCLUDING, BUT NOT LIMITED TO, IMPLIED WARRANTIES OF MERCHANTABILITY, FITNESS FOR A PARTICULAR PURPOSE, AND NON-IN-FRINGEMENT. WE DO NOT GUARANTEE THAT FACEBOOK WILL BE SAFE OR SECURE. FACEBOOK IS NOT RESPONSIBLE FOR THE ACTIONS, CONTENT, INFORMATION, OR DATA OF THIRD PARTIES, AND YOU RELEASE US, OUR DIRECTORS, OFFICERS, EMPLOYEES, AND AGENTS FROM ANY CLAIMS AND DAMAGES, KNOWN AND UNKNOWN, ARISING OUT OF OR IN ANY WAY CONNECTED WITH ANY CLAIM YOU HAVE AGAINST ANY SUCH THIRD PARTIES. IF YOU ARE A CALIFORNIA RESIDENT, YOU WAIVE CALIFORNIA CIVIL CODE §1542, WHICH SAYS: "A GENERAL RELEASE DOES NOT EXTEND TO CLAIMS WHICH THE CREDITOR DOES NOT KNOW OR SUSPECT TO EXIST IN HIS FAVOR AT THE TIME OF EXECUTING THE RELEASE, WHICH IF KNOWN BY HIM MUST HAVE MATERI-ALLY AFFECTED HIS SETTLEMENT WITH THE DEBTOR." WE WILL NOT BE LIABLE TO YOU FOR ANY LOST PROFITS OR OTHER CONSEQUENTIAL, SPECIAL, INDIRECT, OR INCIDENTAL DAMAGES ARISING OUT OF OR IN CONNECTION WITH THIS STATEMENT OR FACEBOOK, EVEN IF WE HAVE BEEN ADVISED OF THE POSSIBILITY OF SUCH DAMAGES. OUR AGGREGATE LIABILITY ARISING OUT OF THIS STATE-MENT OR FACEBOOK WILL NOT EXCEED THE GREATER OF ONE HUNDRED DOLLARS ($100) OR THE AMOUNT YOU HAVE PAID US IN THE PAST TWELVE MONTHS. APPLICABLE LAW MAY NOT ALLOW THE LIMITATION OR EXCLUSION OF LIABILITY OR INCIDENTAL OR CONSEQUENTIAL DAMAGES, SO THE ABOVE LIMITATION OR EXCLUSION MAY NOT APPLY TO YOU. IN SUCH CASES, FACE-BOOK'S LIABILITY WILL BE LIMITED TO THE FULLEST EXTENT PERMITTED BY APPLICABLE LAW.

16. Special Provisions Applicable to Users Outside the United States

We strive to create a global community with consistent standards for everyone, but we also strive to respect local laws. The following provisions apply to users outside the United States:

1. You consent to having your personal data transferred to and processed in the United States.
2. If you are located in a country embargoed by the United States, or are on the U.S. Treasury Department's list of Specially Designated Nationals you will not engage in commercial activities on Facebook (such as advertising or payments) or operate a Platform application or website.
3. Certain specific terms that apply only for German users are available here.

17. Definitions

1. By "Facebook" we mean the features and services we make available, including through (a) our website at www.facebook.com and any other Facebook branded or co-branded websites (including sub-domains, international versions, widgets, and mobile versions); (b) our Platform; (c) social plugins such as the like button, the share button and other similar offerings and (d) other media, software (such as a toolbar), devices, or networks now existing or later developed.
2. By "Platform" we mean a set of APIs and services that enable others, including

application developers and website operators, to retrieve data from Facebook or provide data to us.

3. By "information" we mean facts and other information about you, including actions you take.

4. By "content" we mean anything you post on Facebook that would not be included in the definition of "information."

5. By "data" we mean content and information that third parties can retrieve from Facebook or provide to Facebook through Platform.

6. By "post" we mean post on Facebook or otherwise make available to us (such as by using an application).

7. By "use" we mean use, copy, publicly perform or display, distribute, modify, translate, and create derivative works of.

8. By "active registered user" we mean a user who has logged into Facebook at least once in the previous 30 days.

9. By "application" we mean any application or website that uses or accesses Platform, as well as anything else that receives or has received data from us. If you no longer access Platform but have not deleted all data from us, the term application will apply until you delete the data.

18. Other

1. If you are a resident of or have your principal place of business in the US or Canada, this Statement is an agreement between you and Facebook, Inc. Otherwise, this Statement is an agreement between you and Facebook Ireland Limited. References to "us," "we," and "our" mean either Facebook, Inc. or Facebook Ireland Limited, as appropriate.

2. This Statement makes up the entire agreement between the parties regarding Facebook, and supersedes any prior agreements.

3. If any portion of this Statement is found to be unenforceable, the remaining portion will remain in full force and effect.

4. If we fail to enforce any of this Statement, it will not be considered a waiver.

5. Any amendment to or waiver of this Statement must be made in writing and signed by us.

6. You will not transfer any of your rights or obligations under this Statement to anyone else without our consent.

7. All of our rights and obligations under this Statement are freely assignable by us in connection with a merger, acquisition, or sale of assets, or by operation of law or otherwise.

8. Nothing in this Statement shall prevent us from complying with the law.

9. This Statement does not confer any third party beneficiary rights.

10. You will comply with all applicable laws when using or accessing Facebook.

You may also want to review the following documents:

- Privacy Policy: The Privacy Policy is designed to help you understand how we collect and use information.
- Payment Terms: These additional terms apply to all payments made on or through Facebook.
- Platform Page: This page helps you better understand what happens when you add a third-party application or use Facebook Connect, including how they may access and use your data.

- Facebook Platform Policies: These guidelines outline the policies that apply to applications, including Connect sites.
- Advertising Guidelines: These guidelines outline the policies that apply to advertisements placed on Facebook.
- Promotions Guidelines: These guidelines outline the policies that apply if you have obtained written pre-approval from us to offer contests, sweepstakes, and other types of promotions on Facebook.
- How to Report Claims of Intellectual Property Infringement
- How to Appeal Claims of Copyright Infringement
- Pages Terms

- **To access the Statement of Rights and Responsibilities in several different languages, change the language setting for your Facebook session by clicking on the language link in the left corner of most pages. If the Statement is not available in the language you select, we will default to the English version.**

Facebook • 2011 • English (US)

Updates February 2011
Date of Last Revision: February 10, 2011

Facebook Pages Terms

1. Any user may create a Page; however, only an authorized representative of the subject matter may administer the Page. Pages with names consisting solely of generic or descriptive terms will have their administrative rights removed.

2. Content posted to Pages is public information and is available to everyone.

3. If you collect information from users, you will obtain their consent, make it clear you (and not Facebook) are the one collecting their information, and post a privacy policy explaining what information you collect and how you will use it.

4. You must not build or incorporate any functionality that identifies which users visit your Page.

5. Applications on your Page must comply with the Facebook Platform Policies.

6. You take full responsibility for any sweepstakes, contest, competition or similar offering on your Page and must comply with our Promotions Guidelines.

7. Third party advertisements on Pages are prohibited. Ads or commercial content on Pages must comply with our Advertising Guidelines.

8. You will restrict access to your Page as necessary to comply with all applicable laws and Facebook terms and policies.

9. You may not establish terms beyond those set forth in these terms to govern the posting of content by users on a Page.

10. Page names must:
- a. not consist solely of a generic or descriptive term (e.g. "beer" or "pizza");
- b. use proper, grammatically correct capitalization and may not include excessive capitalization or use all capitals;
- c. not include character symbols, including but not limited to excessive punctuation and trademark designations; and
- d. not include taglines, superfluous descriptions, or unnecessary qualifiers. Campaign names and/or regional or demographic qualifiers are acceptable.

Amended Pages Terms for State & Local Governments in the United States

Government Terms

Amended Pages Terms for State & Local Governments in the United States

If you are a state or local government or government agency in the United States ("You"), and You are using Facebook Pages in your official capacity ("Official Use"), the following terms apply solely to such use and all other terms remain in effect:

1. **Disputes**
You and Facebook will endeavor to resolve any disputes in an amicable fashion.

2. **Venue**
Section 15.1 of the SRR does not apply to your Official Use.
3. **Governing Law**
Section 15.1 of the SRR does not apply to your Official Use.

4. **Indemnity**
If you are a state government or state government agency in the United States:
Section 15.2 of the SRR will apply to You only to the extent expressly permitted by your jurisdiction's laws.

If you are a local government or local government agency in the United States:
Section 15.2 of the SRR will apply to You only to the extent permitted by your jurisdiction's laws.

5. **Disclaimer Requirement**
If you have an official website, your Page must contain, in a prominent location: "If you are looking for more information about [Government Entity], please visit [website URL]."

CHAPTER 6

Resources & Destinations
Great places to visit to obtain more information

Winning applications for 2011 Web 2.0 State and Local Government Awards & Recognition Program

Citizen Engagement

http://www.facebook.com/pages/Help-Rebuild-Fun-Forest-in-Chesapeake-VA/110631095631856

www.fairfaxcounty.gov/news

http://ca-menifee.civicplus.com/requesttracker.aspx

www.denvergov.org/311

http://www.ci.richland.wa.us/list.aspx

http://user.govoutreach.com/arvada/faq.php

http://www3.montgomerycountymd.gov/311/

http://getsatisfaction.com/texasgov/questions/recent

Accountability and Transparency

http://miamidade.gov/wps/portal/Main/ideaMachine/

http://www.pinellascounty.org/etownhall/

Mobile Application

http://www.cctexas.com/ccmobile/

www.m.ca.gov

Innovative Technology

http://nyc.gov/apps/311srmap/

Internal Web 2.0 Advocacy, Coordination and Support

http://www.in.gov/core/subscriptions_main.html

http://www.empire-20.ny.gov/

Public Safety

https://secure.utah.gov/pio/login.html

Economic Development

http://69.31.120.118/sm_parking.xml

Social Media Policies and Guidelines

http://arvada.org/about-arvada/city-terms-and-conditions-of-use/

http://www.bellevuewa.gov/pdf/Manager/Website_Policies_and_Procedures.pdf

http://www.kcmo.org/idc/groups/citymanager/documents/citymanagersoffice/kcbzmonthlyjuly09.pdf.

Administrative Regulation

http://www.cityofchesapeake.net/services/depart/personl/admin_regs/AR126.pdf

Comment Policy

http://www.facebook.com/CityofChesapeake?sk=notes

http://www.facebook.com/topic.php?uid=97157307639&topic=14671

www.smgov.net/uploadedFiles/Main/II-4-16.pdf

www.smgov.net/conditionsofuse

http://howardcountymd.gov/PortalServices/facebook.asp

http://www.catawbacountync.gov/_documents/Social_Networking_Policy-Catawba_County.pdf

http://www.denvergov.org/Portals/534/documents/Web20Policy.pdf

http://www.pinellascounty.org/pdf/social-networking-internet-policy.pdf

http://ocio.ca.gov/Government/IT_Policy/pdf/ITPL_10-02_Social_Media.pdf

http://www.in.gov/ai/appfiles/requests/doc/socialpercent20media.pdf.

http://www.oregon.gov/DAS/EISPD/EGOV/BOARD/social_networking_guide/index.shtml

http://www.texas.gov/en/about/Pages/social-media-policy.aspx

http://www.utahta.wikispaces.net/file/view/Statepercent20ofpercent20Utahpercent-20Socialpercent20Mediapercent20Guidelinespercent209.29.pdf

Federal Government Examples

Milestone	Links
2006	
U.S. Intelligence community launches Intellipedia internal wiki	http://www.collaborationproject.org/display/case/ODNI+Intellipedia/index.html
US Geological Survey updates public about earthquakes via Really Simple Syndication (RSS) feeds	http://webcache.googleusercontent.com/search?q=cache:18q3VaPCv1UJ:earthquake.usgs.gov/recenteqsww/rss.html+USGS+Earthquake+RSS+Feed&cd=1&hl=en&ct=clnk&gl=us&client=firefox-a
2007	
U.S. government channel created on YouTube, puts all government channels in one place	http://www.youtube.com/user/USGovernment
Library of Congress becomes part of small group of government agencies with a blog	http://blogs.loc.gov/loc/archive-by-year/
Transportation Security Administration's IdeaFactory gathers 4,500 security ideas from staff, 20 of which are implemented at the national level	http://www.collaborationproject.org/display/case/Transportation+Security+Administration's+IdeaFactory/
Health and Human Services' Womenshealth.gov becomes the first federal agency on Twitter	http://twitter.com/womenshealth
NASA creates virtual rockets, space stations in Second Life	http://www.space.com/adastra/070526_isdc_second_life.html
Health and Human Services uses Pandemic Flu Leadership Blog to discuss flu on national level	http://www.govtech.com/gt/123185?topic=117677
U.S. government examines "Peer to patent" program, using public participation in patent examination – gets 30,000+ visitors in 126 countries	http://www.collaborationproject.org/display/case/Peer-to-Patent+Project,+US+Patent+and+Trademark+Office/index.html
US Army joins Twitter	http://twitter.com/usarmy

Milestone	Links
DIPNOTE, official State Department blog, launches	http://en.wikipedia.org/wiki/Dipnote
Office of Management and Budget uses Wiki to track earmarks (13,496 collected). Wiki eventually becomes OMB MAX Federal community	http://www.washingtonpost.com/wp-dyn/content/article/2008/01/27/AR2008012701655.html, http://www.whitehouse.gov/omb/assets/omb/financial/max_community_reporting.pdf
2008	
Library of Congress uses Flickr to crowdsource organization of photo archives	http://boingboing.net/2008/01/16/library-of-congress.html
Transportation Security Administration's "Blogger Bob" publicly clears the MacBook Air for airport travel. He will later do the same with the iPad.	http://blog.tsa.gov/2008/03/update-bob-screens-apple-macbook-air.html, http://www.macgasm.net/2010/04/08/blogger-bob-says-your-ipad-has-been-approved-for-travel/
GovLoop founds members-only online federal community	http://en.wikipedia.org/wiki/GovLoop
Department of Defense's Techipedia joins other Gov wikis (State's Diplopedia, FBI Bureaupedia, etc.)	http://www.collaborationproject.org/display/case/DOD+Techipedia/index.html
Coast Guard formally embraces social media like Facebook, YouTube	http://www.collaborationproject.org/display/case/Coast+Guard+Social+Media+Initiative/index.html
Homeland Security sends Hurricane Ike and Gustav response information through MySpace, widgets	http://www.lockergnome.com/inside-weatherbug/2008/09/01/federal-hurricane-response-widgets/
CDCFlu launches on Twitter and gets over 30,000 followers in a week.	http://twitter.com/cdcflu
Apps for Democracy contest launched. 47 applications were built in 30 days, with estimated Return on Investment (ROI) of 4,000percent	http://www.appsfordemocracy.org/about/, http://www.istrategylabs.com/2008/11/apps-for-democracy-yeilds-4000-roi-in-30-days-for-dcgov/
2009	
White House Transparency and Open Government Memo	http://www.whitehouse.gov/the_press_office/TransparencyandOpenGovernment/
Obama Inauguration video on YouTube gets 3 million views in 24 hours	http://www.youtube.com/watch?v=VjnygQ02aW4

Milestone	Links
Obama launches weekly YouTube Address	http://www.washingtontimes.com/blog/ potus-notes/2009/oct/20/the-real-reason-team-obama-uses-video-so-much-its-/
Senate, House launch YouTube channels	http://www.google.com/hostednews/afp/ article/ALeqM5hm26ClGtyz4LsH7y-i0S42ZaCPlWA
Sunlight Labs "Apps for America" Contest offers $5,000 for best government data mashup	http://sunlightlabs.com/contests/ appsforamerica/
The Department of State launches The Sounding Board intranet idea generation forum to enable the 63,000 domestic and overseas employees at the Department of State to submit concrete ideas for improvements to the way the Department does business	http://www.whitehouse.gov/sites/default/ files/microsites/ogi-progress-report-american-people.pdf
FDA creates web widget to track peanut recalls. Within 9 days it is used 1.4 million times	http://www.msnbc.msn.com/id/ 28981756/
General Services Administration signs landmark service agreement with YouTube. Facebook, other social media follow	http://fcw.com/articles/2009/04/29/ gsa-new-media-agreements.aspx
Recovery.gov launched	http://www.recovery.gov/About/Pages/ Recoverygov.aspx
White House gets 92,000 questions from "virtual town meeting"	http://fcw.com/articles/2009/03/30/ obama-virtual-town-hall.aspx
Whitehouse.gov features leading Open Government innovations in "Innovations Gallery"	http://techpresident.com/blog-entry/ white-house-opens-doors-major-open-government-initiatives
Data.gov launches with 47 datasets	http://www.whitehouse.gov/open/ innovations/Data
U.S. Government Launches YouTube Channel	http://www.informationweek.com/news/ government/enterprise-architecture/ showArticle.jhtml?articleID=217600471
NASA launches Spacebook (social workspace/ intranet)	http://www.nasa.gov/centers/goddard/ news/topstory/2009/spacebook.html
Twitter announces verified accounts. CDCE mergency is in the pilot group.	http://mashable.com/2009/06/06/ twitter-verified-accounts/
Chairman of Joint Chiefs of Staff tweets for first time	http://twitter.com/thejointstaff/status/ 3131934563

Milestone	Links
Our Border Network (Homeland Security) creates social network to address border issues	http://www.emergencymgmt.com/safety/Our-Border-Social-Networking-Site-Connects-Public-Federal-Government.html
Department of Justice creates blog	http://blogs.usdoj.gov/blog/page/16
Veterans Affairs "Innovation Initiative" nets 3,000 ideas on improving claims process for Veterans.	http://www4.va.gov/VAI2/VAi2XFAQs.html
Navy creates a virtual world to test submarine design	http://gcn.com/articles/2009/08/24/data-visualization-sidebar-2-navy-sub.aspx
General Services Administration awards contract to increase Federal Cloud Computing services	http://www.datacenterdynamics.com/ME2/dirmod.asp?sid=&nm=&type=news&mod=News&mid=9A02E3B96F2A415A BC72CB5F516B4C10&tier=3&nid=2855C 47E49A3419D9489940DABDDD55A
Department of State launches second Democracy Video Challenge on YouTube and on America.gov in six languages	www.youtube.com/democracychallenge and http://www.state.gov/r/pa/prs/ps/2009/sept/129146.htm
NASA launches open innovation mall challenges using InnoCentive, Yet2.com, and TopCoder	http://www.slsd.jsc.nasa.gov/
Department of State creates Democracy Challenge Facebook page which as of July 2010 has approximately 50,000 users	www.facebook.com/democracychallenge
2010 Census creates blog	http://blogs.census.gov/2010census/page/18/
Whitehouse.gov launches redesigned site using open source software	http://techpresident.com/blog-entry/whitehousegov-goes-drupal
CDC's H1n1 YouTube video gets 2 million views	http://www.youtube.com/watch?v=0wK11 27fHQ4&feature=channel
MIT students win $40,000 in DARPA's "Red Balloon" geolocation contest	http://news.cnet.com/8301-11386_3-10410403-76.html
White House Open Government Directive	www.whitehouse.gov/omb/assets/memoranda_2010/m10-06.pdf
2010	
Social Media plays key role in Haiti earth response – victims located via Twitter + Facebook, people text 'HAITI' to '90999' to make donations	http://washingtontechnology.com/articles/2010/01/14/social-media-haiti-earthquake-relief.aspx

Milestone	Links
General Services Administration Launches Online Public Dialog Tool for 22 agencies. 2000+ ideas and 20,000+ votes collected	http://www.gsa.gov/Portal/gsa/ep/ contentView.do?contentType=GSA_ BASIC&contentId=28995
Obama State of the Union live streamed from White House, Hulu, Facebook, YouTube	http://newteevee.com/2010/01/25/ where-to-watch-obamas-state-of-the-union-address-online/
Department of Defense Unveils Social Media Policy	http://www.defense.gov/NEWS/ DTMpercent2009-026.pdf
NASA employees create OpenGovTracker based on IdeaScale data sets and open API	http://www.cnn.com/2010/US/weather/ 02/05/winter.storm/index.html
NASA Honors 2009 Centennial Challenges Winners – Nine prizes totaling $3.65 million were awarded in 2009	http://www.nasa.gov/home/ hqnews/2010/feb/HQ_M10-030_ Centennial_Challenges.html
White House Guidance on the Use of Challenges and Prizes to Promote Open Government	www.whitehouse.gov/omb/assets/ memoranda_2010/m10-11.pdf
General Services Administration lets public create Public Service Announcement for USA.gov, gives $2,500 prize to Tennessee winner	http://www.federalnewsradio. com/?nid=19&sid=1938566
Agency Open Government Plans submitted	http://www.commondreams.org/ newswire/2010/05/03-0
Library of Congress acquires Twitter's entire archive	http://news.cnet.com/8301-17938_ 105-20002517-1.html
Data.gov's celebrates 1st anniversary, with 270,000+ datasets	data.gov
Office of Management and Budget clarifies Paperwork Reduction Act for agencies, simplifying social media information collections with "Generic Clearances"	http://www.whitehouse.gov/omb/assets/ inforeg/PRA_Gen_ICRs_5-28-2010.pdf
NASA's YouTube channel, with nearly 1,000 videos and 3.5 million views, is more than 8 times more popular than ABC's official YouTube channel	http://www.youtube.com/user/ USGovernment#p/a, http://www.youtube. com/user/abcnetwork?blend=2&ob=4
Department of State announces winners of Democracy Video Challenge 2010. Over 200,000 people voted for the winners and there have been more than 720,000,000 impressions to date	http://www.state.gov/r/pa/prs/ ps/2010/06/143451.htm

Milestone	Links
Barack Obama has 4.2m Twitter followers	http://govtwit.com/stats
Coast Guard seeks oil spill solutions from public, scientists, vendors	http://www.govexec.com/dailyfed/0610/060710rb1.htm
White House memo asks for increased broadband internet resources at Federal level	http://www.whitehouse.gov/the-press-office/presidential-memorandum-unleashing-wireless-broadband-revolution
Updated OMB rules allows government websites to better use social media tools, including Google Analytics and persistent "cookies" to help web users	http://radar.oreilly.com/2010/06/omb-updates-rules-for-cookies.html
White House backs using "Cloud Computing" for speed and savings	http://thehill.com/blogs/hillicon-valley/technology/106761-administration-backs-cloud-computing-while-agencies-weigh-risks
HHS offers money to health care providers if they adopt and "meaningfully use" electronic medical records	http://radar.oreilly.com/2010/07/health-and-human-services-fina.html?utm_source=feedburner&utm_medium=feed&utm_campaign=Feedpercent3A+oreillypercent2Fradarpercent2Fatom+percent28Opercent27Reilly+Radarpercent29
USA.gov's Mobile AppStore puts all Federal apps in one place	http://techpresident.com/blog-entry/uncle-sams-app-store
White House launches 2nd annual SAVE award to collect ideas from Federal employees on how to make government work better	http://techpresident.com/blog-entry/save-award-2010-optimizing-government-inside-out
Department of State Publishes Social Media Policy	http://www.scribd.com/doc/34113752/State-Dept-Social-Media-Policy
GSA's Challenge.gov offers a free platform for agencies to launch their own challenges and contests	Challenge.gov
Gov agencies launch RestoreTheGulf.gov as Federal portal for Deepwater BP oil spill	http://www.restorethegulf.gov/
Department of State launches "Apps 4 Africa" to spur tech innovation in East Africa	http://blogs.state.gov/index.php/site/entry/apps_africa
GovTwit directory of all government agencies, employees and elected officials on Twitter has more than 3,000 members	http://govtwit.com/

Milestone	Links
FEMA to send out emergency alerts via Widgets and Twitter	http://gcn.com/articles/2010/06/23/ fema-pushes-widgets-twitter-for-disaster- preparedness.aspx?s=gcndaily_240610
Federal CIO Vivek Kundra and Craigslist founder Craig Newmark collaborate on government transparency	http://politicalticker.blogs.cnn.com/2010/ 07/09/craigslist-founder-working-with- congress-on-transparency/?fbid=f- wdvdCeS9k
Rep. Charles Djou becomes first Member of Congress use an iPad during a floor speech.	http://politicalticker.blogs.cnn.com/2010/ 06/30/hawaii-republican-makes-ipad- history/?fbid=f-wdvdCeS9k
Defense Dept tries to make submarines internet and cell-phone friendly	http://www.wired.com/dangerroom/ 2010/07/run-wired-run-deep-subs-may- finally-get-online/
NASA Launches Moonbase Alpha, online 3-D educational video game	http://j.mp/cc2qdg

Social Media and Web 2.0 in Government

http://www.usa.gov/webcontent/technology/other_tech.shtml

What Is Social Media and Web 2.0?

Social Media and Web 2.0 define activities that integrate technology, social interaction, and content creation. Social media tools use the "wisdom of crowds" to collaboratively connect online information. Through social media, people or groups can create, organize, edit, comment on, combine, and share content. Social media and Web 2.0 use many technologies and forms, including RSS and other syndicated web feeds, blogs, wikis, photo–sharing, video–sharing, podcasts, social networking, social bookmarking, mashups, widgets, virtual worlds, microblogs, and more.

How to Implement

▶ OMB guidance on Paperwork Reduction Act and use of Social Media (PDF, 83.3 KB, 7 pages, April 2010, requires Adobe Acrobat Reader)

▶ OMB Memorandum 10-23, Guidance for Agency Use of Third-Party Websites and Applications (PDF, 78 KB, 9 pages, June 2010, requires Adobe Acrobat Reader)

- View how–to video for Web managers: How To Use Social Media Strategically in the Federal Government
- Open Government, Transparency, and Social Media Presentation (PDF, 11,490 KB, 87 pages, April 2009, requires Adobe Acrobat Reader)
- Barriers and Solutions to Implementing Social Media and Web 2.0 in Government Recommendations from leaders of the Federal Web Managers Council, December 2008 (PDF, 55 KB, 4 pages, December 2008, requires Adobe Acrobat Reader)
- Examples of Agencies Using Online Content and Technology to Achieve Mission and Goals (PDF, 45 KB, 5 pages, December 2008, requires Adobe Acrobat Reader)
- Matrix of Web 2.0 Technology Tools and Government (PDF, 45 KB, 2 pages, March 2008, requires Adobe Acrobat Reader)
- Social Software and National Security: An Initial Net Assessment (PDF, 527.86 KB, 42 pages, requires Adobe Acrobat Reader), this DoD research paper has applications and implications for the larger government community.

Resources

- Federal Agency Records Officers
- USA.gov and GobiernoUSA.gov's Social Media Style and Editorial Guidelines (PDF, 311 KB, 14 pages, March 2010, requires Adobe Acrobat Reader)
- Flickr Best Practices Guide for Government (PDF, 216 KB, 14 pages, December 2009, requires Adobe Acrobat Reader)
- CDC Social Media Tools Guidelines & Best Practices
- List: Web 2 0 Governance Policies and Best Practices
- Social Media Outlet Authentication Best Practices
- 7 Ways to Promote Your Offline Event Using Social Media
- Social Media Policies database, sorted by Industry
- Guidelines for Secure Use of Social Media by Federal Departments and Agencies
- New Media Across Government (video on YouTube)
- Records Management and Recent Web Technologies
- Past New Media Talks–Free On-Demand Webinars offered by Web Manager University

Endnotes

1. http://www.pewinternet.org/Reports/2010/Government-Online.aspx

2. http://www.itu.int/ITU-D/ict/statistics/

3. http://pewinternet.org/Reports/2010/Government-Online.aspx

4. http://www.fcgov.com/budget/budget-calculator.php

5. http://www.pinellascounty.org/etownhall/

6. http://miamidade.gov/wps/portal/Main/ideaMachine/

7. Cable, Susan, Public Technology Institute, May 2011

8. http://www.facebook.com/pages/Help-Rebuild-Fun-Forest-in-Chesapeake-VA/110631095631856

9. http://blog.udot.utah.gov/

10. http://twitter.com/#!/utdpspio

11. http://twitter.com/#!/corybooker

12. http://www.pewinternet.org/topics/Podcasting.aspx

13. www.fairfaxcounty.gov/news

14. http://a841-tfpweb.nyc.gov/jackson-heights/map/?zoom=16&lat=40.74826&lon=-73.889&layers=B0FFFTFFTTT

15. http://www.denvergov.org/Default.aspx?alias=www.denvergov.org/denver311

16. http://www.in.gov/core/subscriptions.html

17. http://www.ci.richland.wa.us/list.aspx

18. https://alert.montgomerycountymd.gov/index.php?CCheck=1

19. http://www.texas.gov/en/Ask/Pages/live-chat.aspx?AspxAutoDetectCookieSupport=1

20. http://www.cctexas.com/ccmobile/

21. http://ca-menifee.civicplus.com/requesttracker.aspx

22. http://www.smgov.net/departments/transportation/google_parking_mapsv2.aspx?map=all

23. http://www.nyc.gov/html/media/media/PDF/90dayreport.pdf

24. http://www.empire-20.ny.gov/

25. http://www.weboverhauls.com/ce/pressreleases/pr_2010_02_23.htm

26. http://www.androlib.com/android.application.com-awc-tweetassist-retail-xwAw.aspx

27. https://addons.mozilla.org/en-us/firefox/addon/easy-youtube-video-downl-10137/

28. http://accessify.com/tools-and-wizards/accessibility-tools/easy-youtube-caption-creator/

29. http://www.m.ca.gov/

30. http://www.nyc.gov/html/media/media/PDF/90dayreport.pdf

31. http://americancityandcounty.com/technology/using-social-media-metrics-201007/

32. http://ohmygov.com/blogs/general_news/archive/2011/05/09/fema-sees-social-media-as-key-to-emergency-response-efforts.aspx

33. http://www.hsdl.org/?view&doc=108859&coll=limited

34. http://www.howto.gov/social-media

35. Berman, Barbara, Listening to the Public, Adding the Voices of the People to Government Performance Measurement and Reporting, Fund for the City of New York, New York, 2005

36. http://www.nascio.org/newsroom/pressRelease.cfm?id=93